British Railw

CW00591815

LOCOI

SIXTY-SIXTH EDITION
2024

The complete guide to all
Locomotives which operate on
the national railway
and Eurotunnel networks

Robert Pritchard

ISBN 978 1915 984 09 8

© 2023. Platform 5 Publishing Ltd, 52 Broadfield Road, Sheffield, S8 0XJ,
England.

Printed in Engla

CONTENTS

PROVISION OF INFORMATION

This book has been compiled with care to be as accurate as possible, but some information is not easily available and the publisher cannot be held responsible for any errors or omissions. We would like to thank the companies and individuals who have been helpful in supplying information to us. The authors of this series of books are always pleased to receive notification of any inaccuracies that may be found, to enhance future editions. Please send comments to:

Robert Pritchard, Platform 5 Publishing Ltd, 52 Broadfield Road, Sheffield, S8 0XJ, England.

e-mail: robert.pritchard@platform5.com Tel: 0114 255 2625.

This book is updated to information received by 16 October 2023.

UPDATES

This book is updated to the Stock Changes given in **Today's Railways UK 261** (November 2023). The Platform 5 railway magazine **"Today's Railways UK"** publishes Stock Changes every month to update this book. The magazine also contains news and rolling stock information on the railways of Great Britain and is published on the second Monday of every month. For further details of **Today's Railways UK**, please contact Platform 5 Publishing Ltd or visit our website **www.platform5.com**.

Front cover photograph: Platinum Jubilee-liveried 67007 leads a Newbury Racecourse–Westbury VSOE empty stock through Great Bedwyn on 7 June 2023.   **Tony Bartlett**

BRITAIN'S RAILWAY SYSTEM

The structure of Britain's railway system has changed significantly during recent years, following the ongoing Covid-19 pandemic and subsequent drop in passenger numbers. Although passengers have since been returning in numbers, that drop in passengers in 2020 meant that franchises were no longer profitable and the Government was forced to step in and provide financial support to operators. Initially in March 2020 the Transport Secretary suspended rail franchising and operators transitioned to "Emergency Measures Agreements". These EMAs suspended the normal financial agreements, instead transferring all revenue and cost risk to the Government. Operators in England all accepted these new arrangements and continued to operate trains (initially with reduced service frequencies) for a small management fee. Similar arrangements were put in place by the Scottish and Welsh Governments for ScotRail, Caledonian Sleeper and Transport for Wales.

The EMAs initially lasted for six months from which time longer "Emergency Recovery Management Agreements" (ERMAs) were put in place. These were similar management contracts which continued to see operators run services for a management fee. Since then operators have been transitioning to new National Rail Contracts (NRCs). During an NRC operators are paid a fixed management fee of around 1.5% for operating services and additional small performance fees if agreed targets are achieved.

In the longer term a new body called Great British Railways is planned to take over the running of the railways and specifically take over Network Rail's responsibilities as well as some functions currently carried out by the Department for Transport and Rail Delivery Group. The franchise model will be changed to one of concessions, although this will take some years to fully implement.

In London and on Merseyside concessions were already in place. These see the operator paid a fee to run the service, within tightly specified guidelines. Operators running a concession would not normally take commercial risks, although there are usually penalties and rewards in the contract.

Britain's national railway infrastructure is owned by a "not for dividend" company, Network Rail. In 2014 Network Rail was reclassified as a public sector company, being described by the Government as a "public sector arm's-length body of the Department for Transport".

Most stations and maintenance depots are leased to and operated by the Train Operating Companies (TOCs), but some larger stations are controlled by Network Rail. The only exception is the infrastructure on the Isle of Wight: The Island Line franchise uniquely included maintenance of the infrastructure as well as the operation of passenger services. Both the infrastructure and trains are operated by South Western Railway.

Trains are operated by TOCs over Network Rail tracks (termed the National Network), regulated by access agreements between the parties involved. In general, TOCs are responsible for the provision and maintenance of the trains and staff necessary for the direct operation of services, whilst

Network Rail is responsible for the provision and maintenance of the infrastructure and also for staff to regulate the operation of services.

The Department for Transport (DfT) is the authority for the national network. Transport Scotland has operated ScotRail since April 2022 and is also responsible for the Caledonian Sleeper franchises. In February 2021 the Welsh Government took over the operation of the Wales & Borders franchise (Transport for Wales) from KeolisAmey.

Each franchise was set up with the right to run specified services within a specified area for a period of time, in return for the right to charge fares and, where appropriate, to receive financial support from the Government. Subsidy was payable in respect of socially necessary services. Service standards are monitored by the DfT throughout the duration of the franchise. Franchisees earned revenue primarily from fares and from subsidy. They generally leased stations from Network Rail and earned rental income by sub-letting parts of them, for example to retailers.

TOC's and open access operator's main costs are the track access charges they pay to Network Rail, the costs of leasing stations and rolling stock and of employing staff. Franchisees may do light maintenance work on rolling stock or contract it out to other companies. Heavy maintenance is normally carried out by the Rolling Stock Leasing Companies, according to contracts.

DOMESTIC PASSENGER TRAIN OPERATORS

The majority of passenger trains are operated by Train Operating Companies, now supported by the Government through National Rail Contracts. For reference the date of the expiry of the original franchise is also given here (if later than the current NRC expiry date).

Name of franchise	*Operator*	*Trading Name*
Caledonian Sleeper	Scottish Government	**Caledonian Sleeper**

The original Sleeper franchise started in April 2015 when operation of the ScotRail and ScotRail Sleeper franchises was separated. Abellio won the ScotRail franchise and Serco the Caledonian Sleeper franchise. The Scottish Government took over the operation of the Sleeper from Abellio in 2023. Caledonian Sleeper operates four trains nightly between London Euston and Scotland using locomotives hired from GBRf. New CAF Mark 5 rolling stock was introduced during 2019.

Chiltern	Arriva (Deutsche Bahn)	**Chiltern Railways**

NRC until 1 April 2025 with the option to extend to December 2027

Chiltern Railways operates a frequent service between London Marylebone, Oxford, Banbury and Birmingham Snow Hill, with some peak trains extending to Kidderminster. There are also regular services from Marylebone to Stratford-upon-Avon and to Aylesbury Vale Parkway via Amersham (along the London Underground Metropolitan Line). The fleet consists of DMUs of Classes 165, and 168 plus a number of locomotive-hauled rakes used on some of the Birmingham route trains, worked by Class 68s hired from DRS.

Cross Country Arriva (Deutsche Bahn) **CrossCountry**
ERMA until 15 October 2027 with the option to extend to October 2031

CrossCountry operates a network of long distance services between Scotland, the North-East of England and Manchester to the South-West of England, Reading, Southampton, Bournemouth and Guildford, centred on Birmingham New Street. These trains are formed of diesel Class 220/221 Voyagers. Inter-urban services also link Nottingham, Leicester and Stansted Airport with Birmingham and Cardiff. These trains use Class 170 DMUs.

Crossrail MTR **Elizabeth Line**
Concession until 27 May 2025

This concession started in May 2015. Initially Crossrail took over the Liverpool Street–Shenfield stopping service from Greater Anglia, using a fleet of Class 315 EMUs, with the service branded "TfL Rail". The core Crossrail railway in central London started operating in May 2022 and since then the operation has been branded the "Elizabeth Line". Class 345 EMUs are now used on all services running from Reading/Heathrow Airport to Shenfield/Abbey Wood.

East Coast DfT **London North Eastern Railway**
Operated by DfT's "Operator of Last Resort" until June 2025

LNER operates frequent long distance trains on the East Coast Main Line between London King's Cross, Leeds, Lincoln, Harrogate, York, Newcastle-upon-Tyne and Edinburgh, with less frequent services to Bradford, Skipton, Hull, Middlesbrough, Glasgow, Stirling, Aberdeen and Inverness. A fleet of 65 Hitachi Class 800 and 801 "Azuma" trains (a mix of bi-mode and electric, 5- and 9-car units) operate the majority of services. A small number of Class 91 + Mark 4 sets have been retained and are mainly used on Leeds and some York services.

East Midlands Transport UK Group **East Midlands Railway**
NRC until 17 October 2026 with the option to extend to October 2030

EMR operates a mix of long distance high speed services on the Midland Main Line (MML), from London St Pancras to Sheffield, Nottingham (plus peak-hour trains to Lincoln) and Corby, and local and regional services ranging from the long distance Norwich–Liverpool route to Nottingham–Skegness, Nottingham–Mansfield–Worksop, Derby–Matlock and Newark Castle–Crewe. It also operates local services across Lincolnshire. Trains on the MML are worked by a fleet of Class 222 DMUs, whilst the local and regional fleet consists of DMU Classes 158 and 170. Class 360 EMUs operate services on the St Pancras–Corby route.

East Anglia Transport UK Group (60%)/Mitsui Group (40%) **Greater Anglia**
NRC until 19 September 2024 with option for a 2 year extension; original franchise was until 11 October 2025

Greater Anglia operates main line trains between London Liverpool Street, Ipswich and Norwich and local trains across Norfolk, Suffolk and parts of Cambridgeshire. It also runs local and commuter services into Liverpool Street from the Great Eastern (including Southend, Braintree and Clacton) and West Anglia (including Ely/Cambridge and Stansted Airport) routes. In 2019–20 a new fleet of Stadler EMUs and bi-mode units (Classes 745 and 755) was introduced on the GEML and in East Anglia, replacing older DMUs and loco-hauled trains. A large fleet of 133 new 5-car Class 720 Aventras now all other services out of Liverpool Street.

Essex Thameside Trenitalia **c2c**
NRC until 25 July 2025; original franchise was until 10 November 2029

c2c operates an intensive, principally commuter, service from London Fenchurch Street to Southend and Shoeburyness, via both Upminster and Tilbury. The fleet consists of 74 Class 357 EMUs and a fleet of 12 new 5-car Class 720 Aventras.

Great Western
First Group
Great Western Railway

NRC until 21 June 2025 with the option to extend to June 2028

Great Western Railway operates long distance trains from London Paddington to South Wales, the West Country and Worcester and Hereford. In addition, there are frequent trains along the Thames Valley corridor to Newbury/Bedwyn and Oxford, plus local and regional trains throughout the South-West including the Cornish, Devon and Thames Valley branches, the Reading–Gatwick North Downs Line and Cardiff–Portsmouth Harbour and Bristol–Weymouth regional routes. Long distance services are in the hands of a fleet of Class 800/802 bi-mode InterCity Express Trains. DMUs of Classes 165 and 166 are used on the Thames Valley branches and North Downs routes as well as on local services around Bristol and Exeter and across to Cardiff. Class 387 EMUs are used between Paddington, Reading, Didcot Parkway and Newbury. Classes 150, 158, 165 and 166 and a small fleet of short 4-car HSTs are used on local and regional trains in the South-West. A small fleet of Class 57s is maintained to work the overnight "Cornish Riviera" Sleeper service between London Paddington and Penzance formed of Mark 3 coaches.

London Rail
Arriva (Deutsche Bahn)
London Overground

Concession until 3 May 2026

London Overground operates services on the Richmond–Stratford North London Line and the Willesden Junction–Clapham Junction West London Line, plus the East London Line from Highbury & Islington to New Cross and New Cross Gate, with extensions to Clapham Junction (via Denmark Hill), Crystal Palace and West Croydon. It also runs services from London Euston to Watford Junction. All these use Class 378 EMUs, with Class 710s also used on the Watford Junction route. Class 710s operate services on the Gospel Oak–Barking Riverside line. London Overground also operates some suburban services from London Liverpool Street – to Chingford, Enfield Town and Cheshunt. These services mainly use Class 710/1s, with one of these units additionally used on the Romford–Upminster shuttle.

Merseyrail Electrics
Serco (50%)/Transport UK Group (50%)
Merseyrail

Concession until 22 July 2028. Under the control of Merseytravel PTE instead of the DfT
Due to be reviewed every five years to fit in with the Merseyside Local Transport Plan

Merseyrail operates services between Liverpool and Southport, Ormskirk, Kirkby, Hunts Cross, New Brighton, West Kirby, Chester and Ellesmere Port. A new fleet of Class 777 EMUs are currently replacing the Class 507 and 508 EMUs.

Northern
DfT
Northern

Operated by DfT's "Operator of Last Resort" until further notice

Northern operates a range of inter-urban, commuter and rural services throughout the North of England, including those around the cities of Leeds, Manchester, Sheffield, Liverpool and Newcastle. The network extends from Chathill in the north to Nottingham in the south, and Cleethorpes in the east to St Bees in the west. Long distance services include Leeds–Carlisle, Morpeth–Carlisle and York–Blackpool North. The operator uses a large fleet of DMUs of Classes 150, 155, 156, 158, 170 and 195 plus EMU Classes 319, 323, 331 and 333. New fleets of DMUs (Class 195) and EMUs (Class 331) are used on a number of routes, and were followed by Class 769 bi-mode diesel electric units (converted from Class 319s) in 2021.

ScotRail
Scottish Government
ScotRail

Operated by the Scottish Government from April 2022, having taken over ScotRail from Abellio

ScotRail provides almost all passenger services within Scotland and also trains from Glasgow to Carlisle via Dumfries. The company operates a large fleet of DMUs of Classes 156, 158 and 170 and EMU Classes 318, 320, 334, 380 and 385. A fleet of 25 refurbished HSTs have been introduced onto InterCity services between Edinburgh/Glasgow and Aberdeen and Inverness and also between Inverness and Aberdeen. In 2021 five Class 153s were also introduced on the West Highland Line (mainly the Oban line) to provide more capacity and space for bikes and other luggage.

South Eastern	DfT	**Southeastern**

Operated by DfT's "Operator of Last Resort" until further notice.

Southeastern operates all services in the south-east London suburbs, the whole of Kent and part of Sussex, which are primarily commuter services to London. It also operates domestic High Speed trains on HS1 from London St Pancras to Ashford, Ramsgate, Dover and Faversham with additional peak services on other routes. EMUs of Classes 375, 376, 377, 465, 466 and 707 are used, along with Class 395s on the High Speed trains.

South Western	First Group (70%)/MTR (30%)	**South Western Railway**

NRC until 25 May 2025

South Western Railway operates trains from London Waterloo to destinations across the South and South-West including Woking, Basingstoke, Southampton, Portsmouth, Salisbury, Exeter, Reading and Weymouth, as well as suburban services from Waterloo. SWR also runs services between Ryde and Shanklin on the Isle of Wight, from November 2021 using a fleet of five third rail Vivarail Class 484 units (converted former LU D78 stock). The rest of the fleet consists of DMU Classes 158 and 159 and EMU Classes 444, 450, 455 and 458. A new fleet of Bombardier Class 701s are being delivered and should enter service from late 2023.

Thameslink, Southern &	Govia (Go-Ahead/Keolis)	**Govia Thameslink Railway**
Great Northern (TSGN)		

NRC until 1 April 2025 with the option to extend to April 2028

TSGN is the largest operator in Great Britain (the former Southern franchise was combined with Thameslink/Great Northern in 2015). GTR uses four brands: "Thameslink" for trains between Cambridge North, Peterborough, Bedford and Rainham, Sevenoaks, East Grinstead, Brighton, Littlehampton and Horsham via central London and also on the Sutton/Wimbledon loop using Class 700 EMUs. "Great Northern" comprises services from London King's Cross and Moorgate to Welwyn Garden City, Hertford North, Peterborough, Cambridge and King's Lynn using Class 387 and 717 EMUs. "Southern" operates predominantly commuter services between London, Surrey and Sussex and "metro" services in South London, as well as services along the south Coast between Southampton, Brighton, Hastings and Ashford, plus the cross-London service from South Croydon to Milton Keynes. Class 171 DMUs are used on Ashford–Eastbourne and London Bridge–Uckfield services, whilst all other services are in the hands of Class 377 and 700 EMUs. Finally, Gatwick Express operates semi-fast trains between London Victoria, Gatwick Airport and Brighton using Class 387/2 EMUs.

Trans-Pennine Express	DfT	**TransPennine Express**

Operated by DfT's "Operator of Last Resort" until further notice.

TransPennine Express operates predominantly long distance inter-urban services linking major cities across the North of England, along with Edinburgh and Glasgow in Scotland. The main services are Manchester Airport–Saltburn, Liverpool–Hull, Manchester Piccadilly–York–Scarborough and Liverpool–Newcastle/Edinburgh along the North Trans-Pennine route via Huddersfield, Leeds and York, and Liverpool–Manchester Piccadilly–Cleethorpes along the South Trans-Pennine route via Sheffield. TPE also operates Manchester Airport–Edinburgh/Glasgow and Liverpool–Glasgow services. The fleet consists of Class 185 DMUs, plus three new fleets: Class 68s+Mark 5A (which are to be withdrawn in December 2023) used on the Scarborough route, Class 397s used on Manchester Airport/Liverpool–Scotland and Class 802 bi-mode units used mainly on Liverpool–Newcastle/Edinburgh.

Wales & Borders   Welsh Government   **Transport for Wales**
From February 2021 the Welsh Government took direct control of rail service operation. Infrastructure management continues to be managed by KeolisAmey.

Transport for Wales was procured by the Welsh Government and operates a mix of long distance, regional and local services throughout Wales, including the Valley Lines network of lines around Cardiff, and also through services to the English border counties and to Manchester and Birmingham. The fleet consists of DMUs of Classes 150, 153, 158, 170 and 175 and locomotive-hauled Mark 4 sets hauled by Class 67s. Rebuilt Class 230 diesel-battery units are used on the Wrexham–Bidston line and new Stadler (Class 231/398/756) and CAF (Class 197) fleets are being introduced across other routes by 2025.

West Coast Partnership   First Group (70%)/Trenitalia (30%)   **Avanti West Coast**
NRC until 18 October 2026 with the option to extend to October 2032

Avanti West Coast operates long distance services along the West Coast Main Line from London Euston to Birmingham/Wolverhampton, Manchester, Liverpool, Blackpool North and Glasgow/Edinburgh using Class 390 Pendolino EMUs. It also operates Class 221 Voyagers on the Euston–Chester–Holyhead route and a small number of trains from Wolverhampton to Shrewsbury and to Wrexham. New Hitachi Class 805 and 807 units are due into service from 2024.

West Midlands Trains   Transport UK Group (70%)/JR East (15%)/**West Midlands Railway/**
                         Mitsui (15%)   **London Northwestern**
NRC until 19 September 2024 with option to extend to September 2026; original franchise ran until 31 March 2026

West Midlands Trains operates services under two brand names. West Midlands Railway trains are local and regional services around Birmingham, including to Stratford-upon-Avon, Worcester, Hereford, Redditch, Rugeley and Shrewsbury. WMR is managed by a consortium of 16 councils and the Department for Transport. London Northwestern is the brand used for long distance and regional services from London Euston to Northampton and Birmingham/Crewe and also between Birmingham and Liverpool, Bedford–Bletchley and Watford Junction–St Albans Abbey. The fleet consists of DMU Classes 139, 150 and 172 and EMU Classes 319, 323 and 350. New fleets of CAF Class 196 DMUs and Bombardier Class 730 EMUs are being introduced across a number of routes between 2022 and 2025.

NON-FRANCHISED SERVICES

The following operators run non-franchised, or "open access" services (* special seasonal services):

Operator	Trading Name	Route
Heathrow Airport Holdings	Heathrow Express	London Paddington–Heathrow Airport

Heathrow Express is a frequent express passenger service between London Paddington and Heathrow Airport using a sub-fleet of Great Western Railway Class 387 EMUs (operated jointly with GWR).

Hull Trains (part of First)	Hull Trains	London King's Cross–Hull

Hull Trains operates seven trains a day on weekdays from Hull to London King's Cross via the East Coast Main Line. Bi-mode Class 802s were introduced in 2019–20. Two trains in each direction start back from and extend to Beverley.

Grand Central (part of Arriva)	Grand Central	London King's Cross–Sunderland/ Bradford Interchange

Grand Central operates five trains a day from Sunderland and four from Bradford Interchange to London King's Cross using Class 180 or 221 DMUs.

Locomotive Services (TOC)	Locomotive Services	

Locomotive Services runs various excursions across the network using diesel, electric and steam locomotives operating under the brands Saphos Trains (principally steam-hauled trips), Statesman Rail (diesel-locomotive hauled trips and land cruises), Rail Charter Services, Midland Pullman (HST tours using the luxury HST set) and Intercity (mainly electric locomotive-hauled tours).

First East Coast	Lumo	London King's Cross–Edinburgh

Lumo started operating services from London to Edinburgh via the East Coast Main Line in October 2021 and now operates five trains per day using new electric Class 803 units.

North Yorkshire Moors Railway Enterprises	North Yorkshire Moors Railway	Pickering–Grosmont–Whitby/ Battersby, Sheringham–Cromer*

The North Yorkshire Moors Railway operates services on the national network between Grosmont and Whitby as an extension of its Pickering–Grosmont services and also operates services between Sheringham and Cromer on behalf of the North Norfolk Railway.

South Yorkshire Supertram	Stagecoach Supertram	Meadowhall South–Rotherham Parkgate

South Yorkshire Supertram holds a passenger licence to allow the operation of the pilot tram-train service linking Sheffield city centre with Rotherham Central and Rotherham Parkgate.

Tyne & Wear PTE	Tyne & Wear Metro	Pelaw–Sunderland

Tyne & Wear Passenger Transport Executive holds a passenger license to allow the operation of its Metro service over Network Rail tracks between Pelaw and Sunderland.

Vintage Trains	Vintage Trains	Birmingham Snow Hill–Stratford-upon-Avon*

Vintage Trains operates steam-hauled services on a seasonal basis.

West Coast Railway Company	West Coast Railway Company	Fort William–Mallaig* York–Settle–Carlisle* Carnforth–York–Scarborough*

WCRC operates steam-hauled services on these routes on a seasonal basis and a range of other excursions across the network, including the Northern Belle luxury train.

INTERNATIONAL PASSENGER OPERATORS

Eurostar International operates passenger services between London St Pancras and mainland Europe. The company, established in 2010, is jointly owned by SNCF (the national operator of France): 55%, SNCB (the national operator of Belgium): 5% and Patina Rail: 40%. Patina Rail is made up of Canadian-based Caisse de dépôt et placement du Québec (CDPG) and UK-based Hermes Infrastructure (owning 30% and 10% respectively). This 40% was previously owned by the UK Government until it was sold in 2015.

In addition, a service for the conveyance of accompanied road vehicles through the Channel Tunnel is provided by the tunnel operating company, Eurotunnel. All Eurotunnel services are operated in top-and-tail mode by the powerful Class 9 Bo-Bo-Bo locomotives.

FREIGHT TRAIN OPERATORS

The following operators operate freight services or empty passenger stock workings under "Open Access" arrangements:

Colas Rail: Colas Rail operates a number of On-Track Machines and also supplies infrastructure monitoring trains for Network Rail. It also operates a number of different freight flows, including oil and timber. Colas Rail has a small but varied fleet consisting of Class 37s, 56s, 66s and 70s. It also uses HST power cars (Class 43) on some Network Rail test trains.

DB Cargo (UK): The biggest freight operator in the country, DBC (EWS until bought by Deutsche Bahn, when it was initially called DB Schenker) provides a large number of infrastructure trains to Network Rail and also operates coal, steel, intermodal and aggregate trains nationwide. The core fleet is Class 66s. Of the original 250 ordered, 69 are currently working with DB's French and Polish operations, although some of the French locos do return to the UK when major maintenance is required and others have returned to the UK permanently. A small pool of around six Class 60s are also used on some of the heavier trains, the remainder of the fleet having been stored or sold, although DB Cargo is still responsible for the maintenance of GBRf and DCR Class 60s at Toton.

DBC's fleet of Class 67s are used on passenger or standby duties for Transport for Wales and LNER and also on excursions or special trains. The Class 90s have all now been stored and the Class 92s are mainly used on a limited number of overnight freights on High Speed 1.

DBC also operates the Class 325 EMUs for Royal Mail and a number of excursion trains.

Devon & Cornwall Railways (part of Cappagh Construction Contractors (London)): DCRail specialises in short-term freight haulage contracts, using Class 56s or four Class 60s acquired from DB Cargo. It has also purchased a number of other Class 60s, some of which will be returned to service.

Direct Rail Services: DRS has built on its original nuclear flask traffic to operate a number of different services. The main flows are intermodal plus the provision of crews and locomotives to Network Rail for autumn RailHead Treatment Trains and also infrastructure trains. DRS has a varied fleet of locomotives, with Class 37s, 57s and 66s working alongside the more modern Class 68s and diesel-electric Class 88s. Class 68s are hired to Chiltern Railways and TransPennine Express for passenger work.

Freightliner: Freightliner (owned by Genesee & Wyoming) operates container trains from the main Ports at Southampton, Felixstowe, Tilbury and London Gateway to major cities including London, Manchester, Leeds and Birmingham. It also operates trains of coal, cement, infrastructure and aggregates. Most services are worked by Class 66s, with Class 70s mainly used on some of the heavier intermodal trains and cement trains from the Peak District. A fleet of Class 90 electrics are used on intermodal trains on the Great Eastern and West Coast Main Lines, this includes 13 locomotives previously operated by Greater Anglia.

The six Class 59/2s were purchased from DB Cargo and are used alongside the Mendip Rail 59/0s and 59/1s on stone traffic from the Mendip quarries and around the South-East.

GB Railfreight: GBRf (owned by Infracapital) operates a mixture of traffic types, mainly using Class 66s together with a small fleet of Class 73s on infrastructure duties and test trains in the South-East and ten Class 60s acquired from Colas Rail in 2018. The company has also now purchased a number of Class 56s and owns a single Class 59, 59003. Most of the Class 56s are being rebuilt as Class 69s with a new GM engine. A fleet of Class 92s is also used on some intermodal flows to and from Dollands Moor or through the Channel Tunnel to Calais. Traffic includes coal, intermodal, biomass, aggregates and gypsum as well as infrastructure services for Network Rail and London Underground. GBRf also supplies various locomotives, including Classes 66, 73/9 and 92 to work the Caledonian Sleeper and owns the three former Colas Rail Class 47s.

GBRf operates some excursion trains, including those using the preserved Class 201 "Hastings" DEMU.

LORAM (UK): LORAM has a freight license and operates a limited number of trains, most hauling On-Track Machines using hired-in locomotives operating on behalf of Network Rail.

Rail Adventure: This German based company now has a UK license and has rebuilt some former Grand Central/East Midlands HST power cars for stock movements. In 2022 the company took over Birmingham based train operating company SLC Operations which operates a number of contracts for Network Rail.

Rail Operations Group: This company mainly facilitates rolling stock movements by providing drivers or using locomotives hired from other companies or by using Class 37s hired from Europhoenix. It has also operated trails using Class 319 and 768 bi-mode units on parcels logistics services under its **Orion** subsidiary. ROG has also operated test trains for Data Acquisition & Testing Services.

Varamis Rail: This new operator obtained an operating license in 2022 and has been operating a Class 321 converted to carry parcels. A new service started linking Birmingham with Glasgow in 2022.

West Coast Railway Company: WCRC has a freight licence but doesn't operate any freight as such – only empty stock movements. Its fleet of Class 47s, supplemented by steam locomotives and a smaller number of Class 33s, 37s and 57s, is used on excursion work nationwide.

In addition, Amey, Balfour Beatty Rail, Harsco Rail, Swietelsky Babcock Rail (SB Rail) and VolkerRail operate trains formed of On-Track Machines.

INTRODUCTION

This book contains details of all locomotives which can run on Britain's national railway network, plus those of Eurotunnel.

Locomotives currently approved for use on the national railway network fall into four broad types: passenger, freight, mixed traffic and shunting.

Passenger

The number of dedicated passenger locomotives has not changed significantly in recent years. Classes 43 (HST) and 91 and some members of Classes 57, 67, 68, 73/9 and 92 are dedicated to franchised and Open Access passenger operations. Excursion trains have a few dedicated locomotives but mainly use locomotives that are best described as mixed traffic.

Freight

By far the most numerous locomotives are those used solely for bulk commodity and intermodal freight. Since 1998 a large number of new Class 66 locomotives have replaced many former BR designs and in more recent years smaller numbers of Class 70s have also been introduced. There are however a significant number of BR era Class 20, 37, 47, 50, 56, 60, 73/1, 86, 90 and 92 locomotives still in use; their number has increased slightly as some locomotives have been reinstated to cope with demand. In addition, there is a small fleet of Class 59s acquired privately in the 1980s and 1990s and a small number of re-engined Class 57s in use.

Mixed Traffic

In addition to their use on passenger and commodity freight workings these locomotives are used for stock movements and specialist infrastructure and test trains. The majority, but not all, are fitted with Electric Train Supply. Locomotives from Classes 20, 33, 37, 47, 57, 67, 68, 73/9, 88 and 90 fall into this category. Also included under this heading are preserved locomotives permitted to operate on the national railway network. Although these have in the past solely operated excursion trains they are increasingly seeing occasional use on other types of trains. Some, such as Class 50s with GB Railfreight, are frequently used by the main freight companies.

Shunting

Very few shunting locomotives are now permitted to operate freely on the National Railway network. The small number that are have to be fitted with a plethora of safety equipment in order to have engineering acceptance. They are mainly used for local workings such as trips between yards or stock movements between depots and stations. Otherwise, shunting locomotives are not permitted to venture from depots or yards onto the National Railway network other than into defined limits within interface infrastructure. Remotely-controlled driverless shunters are not included in this book. However, all ex-BR shunting locomotives are listed under Section 1.1 "Diesel Shunting Locomotives".

Locomotives which are owned by, for example, DB Cargo or Freightliner, which have been withdrawn from service and are awaiting disposal are listed in the main part of the book. Locomotives which are awaiting disposal at scrapyards are listed in the "Locomotives Awaiting Disposal" section.

Only preserved locomotives which are currently passed for operation on the National Railway network are included. Others, which may still be Network Rail registered but not at present certified for use, are not included, but can be found in the Platform 5 book, "Preserved Locomotives of British Railways".

LAYOUT OF INFORMATION

Locomotive classes are listed in numerical order of class. Principal details and dimensions are quoted for each class in metric and/or imperial units as considered appropriate bearing in mind common UK usage.

The heading "Total" indicates how many of that particular class are listed in this book.

Where numbers actually carried are different from those officially allocated, these are noted in class headings where appropriate. Where locomotives have been recently renumbered, the most immediate previous number is shown in parentheses. Each entry is laid out as in the following example:

No.	Detail	Livery	Owner	Pool		Allocn.	Name
60055 +	**DC**	DC	DCRO		TO		Thomas Barnado

Detail Differences. Only detail differences which currently affect the areas and types of train which locomotives may work are shown. Where such differences occur within a class or part class, they are shown in the "Detail" column alongside the individual locomotive number.

Codes: Codes are used to denote the livery, owner, pool and depot of each locomotive. Details of these will be found in section 6 of this book.

The owner is the responsible custodian of the locomotive and this may not always be the legal owner. Actual ownership can be very complicated. Some vehicles are owned by finance/leasing companies. Others are owned by subsidiary companies of a holding company or by an associate company of the responsible custodian or operator.

Depot allocation codes for all locomotives are shown in this book (apart from shunting locomotives where the actual location of each is shown). It should be noted that today much locomotive maintenance is undertaken away from these depots. This may be undertaken at fuelling points, berthing sidings or similar, or by mobile maintenance teams. Therefore locomotives in particular may not return to their "home" depots as often as in the past.

(S) denotes that the locomotive is stored (the actual location is shown).

Names: Only names carried with official sanction are listed. Names are shown in UPPER/lower case characters as actually shown on the name carried on the locomotive.

GENERAL INFORMATION

CLASSIFICATION AND NUMBERING

All locomotives are classified and allocated numbers under the TOPS numbering system, introduced in 1972. This comprises a two-digit class number followed by a three-digit serial number.

For diesel locomotives, class numbers offer an indication of engine horsepower as shown in the table below.

Class No. Range	Engine hp
01–14	0–799
15–20	800–1000
21–31	1001–1499
32–39	1500–1999
40–54, 57	2000–2999
55–56, 58–70	3000+

For electric locomotives class numbers are allocated in ascending numerical order under the following scheme:

Class 71–80   Direct current and DC/diesel dual system locomotives.
Class 81 onwards   Alternating current and AC/DC dual system locomotives.

Numbers in the 89101–89999 series are allocated to locomotives which have been deregistered but subsequently re-registered for use on the national railway network and whose original number has already been reused. These numbers are normally only carried inside locomotive cabs and are not carried externally in normal circumstances.

WHEEL ARRANGEMENT

For main line locomotives the number of driven axles on a bogie or frame is denoted by a letter (A = 1, B = 2, C = 3) and the number of non-powered axles is denoted by a number. The use of the letter "o" after a letter indicates each axle is individually powered, whilst the "+" symbol indicates bogies are inter-coupled.

For shunting locomotives, the Whyte notation is used. In this notation the number of leading wheels are given, followed by the number of driving wheels and then the trailing wheels.

UNITS OF MEASUREMENT

All dimensions and weights are quoted for locomotives in an "as new" condition with all necessary supplies (eg oil, water and sand) on board. Dimensions are quoted in the order length x width. Lengths quoted are over buffers or couplers as appropriate. All widths are quoted as maxima. Where two different wheel diameter dimensions are shown, the first refers to powered wheels and the second refers to non-powered wheels. All weights are shown as metric tonnes (t = tonnes).

HAULAGE CAPABILITY OF DIESEL LOCOMOTIVES

The haulage capability of a diesel locomotive depends upon three basic factors:

1. Adhesive weight. The greater the weight on the driving wheels, the greater the adhesion and more tractive power can be applied before wheelslip occurs.

2. The characteristics of its transmission. To start a train the locomotive has to exert a pull at standstill. A direct drive diesel engine cannot do this, hence the need for transmission. This may be mechanical, hydraulic or electric. The present British Standard for locomotives is electric transmission. Here the diesel engine drives a generator or alternator and the current produced is fed to the traction motors. The force produced by each driven wheel depends on the current in its traction motor. In other words, the larger the current, the harder it pulls. As the locomotive speed increases, the current in the traction motor falls, hence the *Maximum Tractive Effort* is the maximum force at its wheels the locomotive can exert at a standstill. The electrical equipment cannot take such high currents for long without overheating. Hence the *Continuous Tractive Effort* is quoted which represents the current which the equipment can take continuously.

3. The power of its engine. Not all power reaches the rail, as electrical machines are approximately 90% efficient. As the electrical energy passes through two such machines (the generator or alternator and the traction motors), the *Power at Rail* is approximately 81% (90% of 90%) of the engine power, less a further amount used for auxiliary equipment such as radiator fans, traction motor blowers, air compressors, battery charging, cab heating, Electric Train Supply (ETS) etc. The power of the locomotive is proportional to the tractive effort times the speed. Hence when on full power there is a speed corresponding to the continuous tractive effort.

HAULAGE CAPABILITY OF ELECTRIC LOCOMOTIVES

Unlike a diesel locomotive, an electric locomotive does not develop its power on board and its performance is determined only by two factors, namely its weight and the characteristics of its electrical equipment. Whereas a diesel locomotive tends to be a constant power machine, the power of an electric locomotive varies considerably. Up to a certain speed it can produce virtually a constant tractive effort. Hence power rises with speed according to the formula given in section three above, until a maximum speed is reached at which tractive effort falls, such that the power also falls. Hence the power at the speed corresponding to the maximum tractive effort is lower than the maximum speed.

BRAKE FORCE

Brake Force (also known as brake power) is a measure of the braking power of a locomotive. The Brake Force available is dependant on the adhesion between the rail and the wheels being braked and the normal reaction of the rail on the wheels being braked (and hence on the weight per braked wheel). A locomotive's Brake Force is shown on its data panels so operating staff can ensure sufficient brake power is available for specific trains.

ELECTRIC TRAIN SUPPLY (ETS)

A number of locomotives are equipped to provide a supply of electricity to the train being hauled to power auxiliaries such as heating, cooling fans, air conditioning and kitchen equipment. ETS is provided from the locomotive by means of a separate alternator (except Class 33 locomotives, which have a DC generator). The ETS index of a locomotive is a measure of the electrical power available for train supply. Class 55 locomotives provide an ETS directly from one of their traction generators into the train supply.

Similarly, most locomotive-hauled carriages also have an ETS index, which in this case is a measure of the power required to operate equipment mounted in the carriage. The sum of the ETS indices of all the hauled vehicles in a train must not exceed the ETS index of the locomotive.

ETS is commonly (but incorrectly) known as ETH (Electric Train Heating), which is a throwback to the days before locomotive-hauled carriages were equipped with electrically powered auxiliary equipment other than for train heating.

ROUTE AVAILABILITY (RA)

This is a measure of a railway vehicle's axle load. The higher the axle load of a vehicle, the higher the RA number on a scale from 1 to 10. Each Network Rail route has a RA number and in general no vehicle with a higher RA number may travel on that route without special clearance.

MULTIPLE WORKING

Multiple working between vehicles (ie two or more powered vehicles being driven from one cab) is facilitated by jumper cables connecting the vehicles. However, not all types of locomotive are compatible with each other, and a number of different systems are in use. Some are compatible with others, some are not. BR used "multiple working codes" to designate which locomotives were compatible. The list below shows which classes of locomotives are compatible with each other – the former BR multiple working code being shown in brackets. It should be noted that some locomotives have had the equipment removed or made inoperable.

With other classes:
Classes 20, 25, 31, 33, 37 40 & 73/1*. (Blue Star)
Classes 56 & 58. (Red Diamond)
Classes 59, 66, 67, 68, 70, 73/9 & 88.
* DRS adapted the systems so its Classes 20/3, 37 & 57 could work with each other only.

With other members of same class only:
Class 43, Class 47 (Green Circle), Class 50 (Orange Square), Class 60.

PUSH-PULL OPERATION

Some locomotives are modified to operate passenger and service (formed of laboratory, test and inspection carriages) trains in "push-pull" mode – which allows the train to be driven from either end – either with locomotives at each end (both under power) or with a driving brake van at one end and a locomotive at the other. Various different systems are now in use. Electric locomotive Classes 86, 87, 90 & 91 use a time-division multiplex (TDM) system for push-pull working which utilises the existing Railway Clearing House (RCH) jumper cables fitted to carriages. Previously these cables had only been used to control train lighting and public address systems.

More recently locomotives of Classes 67 and 68 have used the Association of American Railroads (AAR) system.

ABBREVIATIONS

Standard abbreviations used in this book are:

a	Train air brake equipment only.
b	Drophead buckeye couplers.
c	Scharfenberg couplers.
d	Fitted with retractable Dellner couplers.
e	European Railway Traffic Management System (ERTMS) signalling equipment fitted.
k	Fitted with Swinghead Automatic "buckeye" combination couplers.
p	Train air, vacuum and electro-pneumatic brakes.
r	Radio Electric Token Block signalling equipment fitted.
s	Slow Speed Control equipment.
v	Train vacuum brake only.
x	Train air and vacuum brakes ("Dual brakes").
+	Additional fuel tank capacity.

In all cases use of the above abbreviations indicates the equipment in question is normally operable. The definition of non-standard abbreviations and symbols is detailed in individual class headings.

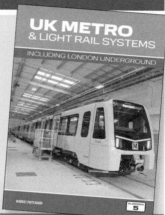

1.1. DIESEL SHUNTING LOCOMOTIVES

All BR design shunting locomotives still in existence, apart from those considered to be preserved, are listed together in this section. Preserved shunting locomotives are listed in the Platform 5 publication "Preserved Locomotives of British Railways" (a small number are listed in both that book and in this publication).

Few shunting locomotives have engineering acceptance and are equipped to operate on Network Rail infrastructure (beyond interface infrastructure), but those that are known to be permitted are indicated here.

For shunting locomotives, instead of the two-letter depot code, actual locations at the time of publication are given. Pool codes for shunting locomotives are not shown.

CLASS 03   BR/GARDNER   0-6-0

Built: 1958–62 by BR at Swindon or Doncaster Works.
Engine: Gardner 8L3 of 152 kW (204 hp) at 1200 rpm.
Transmission: Mechanical. Fluidrive type 23 hydraulic coupling to Wilson-Drewry CA5R7 gearbox with SCG type RF11 final drive.
Maximum Tractive Effort: 68 kN (15300 lbf).
Continuous Tractive Effort: 68 kN (15300 lbf) at 3.75 mph.
Train Brakes: Air & vacuum.

Brake Force: 13 t.	**Dimensions:** 7.93 x 2.59 m.
Weight: 31.3 t.	**Wheel Diameter:** 1092 mm.
Design Speed: 28.5 mph.	**Maximum Speed:** 28.5 mph.
Fuel Capacity: 1364 litres.	**Route Availability:** 1.
Train Supply: Not equipped.	**Total:** 2.

Number   Notes Livery Owner Location

Number	Notes	Livery	Owner	Location
03084		G	WC	West Coast Railway Company, Carnforth Depot
D2381	v	G	WC	West Coast Railway Company, Carnforth Depot (S)

CLASS 07   BR/RUSTON & HORNSBY   0-6-0

Built: 1962 by Ruston & Hornsby, Lincoln.
Engine: Paxman 6RPHL Mk III of 205 kW (275 hp) at 1360 rpm.
Transmission: Electric. One AEI RTB 6652 traction motor.
Maximum Tractive Effort: 126 kN (28240 lbf).
Continuous Tractive Effort: 71 kN (15950 lbf) at 4.38 mph.
Train Brakes: Vacuum.

Brake Force:	**Dimensions:** 8.17 x 2.59 m.
Weight: 43.6 t.	**Wheel Diameter:** 1067 mm.
Design Speed: 20 mph.	**Maximum Speed:** 20 mph.
Fuel Capacity: 1400 litres.	**Train Supply:** Not equipped.
Total: 1.	

07007	v	B	AF	Arlington Fleet Services, Eastleigh Works, Hants

Other number or name carried: 2991 Bruce

CLASS 08   BR/ENGLISH ELECTRIC   0-6-0

Built: 1955–62 by BR at Crewe, Darlington, Derby Locomotive, Doncaster or Horwich Works.
Engine: English Electric 6KT of 298 kW (400 hp) at 680 rpm.
Main Generator: English Electric 801.
Traction Motors: Two English Electric 506.
Maximum Tractive Effort: 156 kN (35000 lbf).
Continuous Tractive Effort: 49 kN (11100 lbf) at 8.8 mph.

Power at Rail: 194 kW (260 hp).	**Train Brakes:** Air & vacuum.
Brake Force: 19 t.	**Dimensions:** 8.92 x 2.59 m.
Weight: 49.6–50.4 t.	**Wheel Diameter:** 1372 mm.
Design Speed: 20 mph.	**Maximum Speed:** 15 mph.
Fuel Capacity: 3037 litres.	**Route Availability:** 5.
Train Supply: Not equipped.	**Total:** 172.

* Locomotives with engineering acceptance to operate on Network Rail infrastructure. 08850 has acceptance for use between Grosmont and Whitby only, for rescue purposes.

§ 08308 has been converted into a battery powered prototype by Positive Traction as part of the "08e" project.

† – Fitted with remote control equipment.

Non-standard liveries:

08308	Green & silver "08e".
08401	Dark green.
08442	Dark grey lower bodyside & light grey upper bodyside.
08445	Yellow, blue & green.
08447	Lilac.
08502	Mid blue.
08568	Dark grey lower bodyside & light grey upper bodyside. Red solebar stripe.
08598	Yellow.
08600	Red with a light grey roof.
08630	Black with red cabsides and solebar stripe.
08645	All over black with a white cross.
08682	Multi-coloured.
08730	ABP Ports blue
08774	Red with a light grey roof.
08899	Crimson lake.
08956	Serco Railtest dark green.

Number	Notes	Livery	Owner	Location
08220	v	**B**	EE	Nottingham Transport Heritage Centre, Ruddington
08308	a	**0**	RL	Barrow Hill Roundhouse, Chesterfield, Derbys
08331		**K**	20	Midland Railway-Butterley, Derbyshire
08375	a	**RL**	RL	Victoria Group, Port of Boston, Boston
08389	at	**E**	HN	Celsa Steel UK, Tremorfa Steelworks, Cardiff
08401	a	**0**	ED	Hunslet Engine Company, Barton-under-Needwood, Staffs
08405	at	**E**	RS	Northern, Neville Hill Depot, Leeds
08410	* a	**GW**	AD	AV Dawson, Ayrton Rail Terminal, Middlesbrough

08411	a	B	RS	RSS, Rye Farm, Wishaw, Sutton Coldfield (S)
08417	* a	Y	HN	Barrow Hill Roundhouse, Chesterfield, Derbys (S)
08418	a	E	WC	West Coast Railway Company, Carnforth Depot (S)
08423	a	RL	RL	PD Ports, Teesport, Grangetown, Middlesbrough
08428	ak	E	HN	Barrow Hill Roundhouse, Chesterfield, Derbys (S)
08441	* a	RS	RS	Greater Anglia, Crown Point Depot, Norwich
08442	a	O	AV	RSS, Rye Farm, Wishaw, Sutton Coldfield (S)
08445	a	O	ED	Daventry International Railfreight Terminal, Crick
08447	a	O	RU	Assenta Rail, Hamilton, Glasgow (S)
08451	*	B	AM	Alstom, Polmadie Depot, Glasgow
08454	*	B	AM	Alstom, Widnes Technology Centre, Cheshire
08460	a	RS	RS	GB Railfreight, Bescot Yard
08472	* a	WA	ED	Reid Freight, Longton, Stoke-on-Trent
08480	* a	RS	RS	Freightliner, Felixstowe FLT
08483	* a	K	LS	L&NWR Heritage Company, Crewe Diesel Depot
08484	a	RS	RS	Greater Anglia, Crown Point Depot, Norwich
08485	a	B	WC	West Coast Railway Company, Carnforth Depot
08499	a	B	TW	Transport for Wales, Canton Depot, Cardiff
08500		E	HN	HNRC, Worksop Depot, Nottinghamshire (S)
08502		O	HN	East Kent Light Railway, Shepherdswell, Kent (S)
08507	a	RB	RS	GB Railfreight, Whitemoor Yard, March, Cambs
08511	a	RS	RS	GB Railfreight, Eastleigh East Yard
08516	a	AW	RS	Arriva TrainCare, Bristol Barton Hill Depot
08523	*	B	RL	EMD, Longport Works, Stoke-on-Trent
08525		ST	EM	Northern, Neville Hill Depot, Leeds (S)
08527		FA	HN	Barrow Hill Roundhouse, Chesterfield, Derbys (S)
08530	*	FL	FL	Hunslet Engine Company, Barton-under-Needwood, Staffs (S)
08531	* a	FH	FL	Nemesis Rail, Burton-on-Trent, Staffordshire
08536		B	RS	RSS, Rye Farm, Wishaw, Sutton Coldfield (S)
08567		AG	AF	Arlington Fleet Services, Eastleigh Works
08568		O	RS	RSS, Rye Farm, Wishaw, Sutton Coldfield (S)
08571	* a	WA	ED	Barrow Hill Roundhouse, Chesterfield, Derbys (S)
08573		K	RL	Weardale Railway, Wolsingham, County Durham
08575		FL	FL	Nemesis Rail, Burton-on-Trent, Staffordshire (S)
08578		E	HN	HNRC, Worksop Depot, Nottinghamshire (S)
08580	*	RS	RS	RSS, Rye Farm, Wishaw, Sutton Coldfield
08585	*	FG	FL	Freightliner, Trafford Park FLT
08588		RL	RL	Alstom, Ilford Works, London
08593		E	RS	RSS, Rye Farm, Wishaw, Sutton Coldfield (S)
08596	* a†	WA	ED	Cockshute Sidings, Stoke-on-Trent
08598		O	AD	AV Dawson, Ayrton Rail Terminal, Middlesbrough
08600	a	O	AD	AV Dawson, Ayrton Rail Terminal, Middlesbrough
08602		B	HN	HNRC, Worksop Depot, Nottinghamshire (S)
08605	†	IC	RS	Willesden Euroterminal Stone Terminal, London
08611	*	B	AM	Alstom, Wembley Depot, London
08613		RL	RL	PD Ports, Teesport, Grangetown, Middlesbrough
08615	*	HU	ED	Hunslet Engine Company, Barton-under-Needwood, Staffs
08616		LM	WM	West Midlands Trains, Tyseley Depot, Birmingham
08617	*	B	AM	Alstom, Oxley Depot, Wolverhampton
08622		K	RL	Hanson Cement, Ketton Cement Works, nr Stamford
08623		DB	HN	HNRC, Worksop Depot, Nottinghamshire (S)

08624	*	**FG**	FL	Freightliner, Felixstowe FLT
08629		**KB**	RS	RSS, Rye Farm, Wishaw, Sutton Coldfield
08630	†	**0**	HN	Celsa Steel UK, Tremorfa Steelworks, Cardiff
08631		**B**	LS	L&NWR Heritage Company, Crewe Diesel Depot
08632	†	**RS**	RS	GB Railfreight, Peterborough Depot
08641	*	**B**	GW	Great Western Railway, Laira Depot, Plymouth
08643		**B**	ED	Aggregate Industries, Merehead Rail Terminal
08644	*	**B**	GW	Great Western Railway, Laira Depot, Plymouth
08645	*	**0**	GW	Great Western Railway, Long Rock Depot, Penzance
08648	*	**K**	RL	ScotRail, Inverness Depot
08649		**KB**	ME	Gemini Rail Group, Wolverton Works, Milton Keynes (S)
08650		**B**	MR	Hanson Aggregates, Whatley Quarry, near Frome
08652		**B**	RS	RSS, Rye Farm, Wishaw, Sutton Coldfield (S)
08653		**E**	HN	Shackerstone, Battlefield Line (S)
08663	* a	**B**	HH	Avon Valley Railway
08669	* a	**WA**	ED	Wabtec Rail, Doncaster Works
08670	* a	**RS**	RS	GB Railfreight, Bescot Yard
08676		**E**	HN	East Kent Light Railway, Shepherdswell, Kent (S)
08678	a	**WC**	WC	West Coast Railway Company, Carnforth Depot
08682		**0**	HN	Shackerstone, Battlefield Line (S)
08683	*	**RS**	RS	GB Railfreight, Eastleigh East Yard
08685		**E**	HN	Barrow Hill Roundhouse, Chesterfield, Derbys (S)
08690		**ST**	EM	Northern, Neville Hill Depot, Leeds (S)
08691	*	**FG**	FL	Freightliner, Ipswich Depot
08696	* a	**B**	AM	Alstom, Wembley Depot, London
08700		**B**	RL	Alstom, Ilford Works, London
08701	a	**RX**	HN	Shackerstone, Battlefield Line (S)
08703	a	**GB**	RS	RSS, Rye Farm, Wishaw, Sutton Coldfield
08704		**RB**	RV	DB Cargo UK, Knottingley Depot
08706	†	**E**	RS	Garston Car Terminal, Liverpool
08709		**E**	RS	RSS, Rye Farm, Wishaw, Sutton Coldfield (S)
08711	k	**RX**	HN	Nemesis Rail, Burton-on-Trent, Staffordshire (S)
08714		**E**	HN	HNRC, Worksop Depot, Nottinghamshire (S)
08721	*	**B**	AM	Alstom, Widnes Technology Centre, Cheshire
08724	*	**WA**	ED	Wabtec Rail, Doncaster Works
08730		**0**	RS	European Metal Recycling, Kingsbury, nr Tamworth
08735	†	**AW**	AV	Arriva TrainCare, Eastleigh Depot
08737		**G**	LS	L&NWR Heritage Company, Southall Depot
08738		**RS**	RS	Freightliner, Felixstowe FLT
08742	†	**RX**	HN	Barrow Hill Roundhouse, Chesterfield, Derbys (S)
08743		**B**	SU	SembCorp Utilities UK, Wilton, Middlesbrough
08752	†	**RS**	RS	Imerys Minerals, Goonbarrow
08754	*	**RL**	RL	Gemini Rail Group, Wolverton Works, Milton Keynes
08756		**RL**	RL	LORAM, Derby
08757		**RG**	PO	Telford Steam Railway
08762		**RL**	RL	Allelys, Studley, Warwickshire
08764	*	**B**	AM	Alstom, Polmadie Depot, Glasgow
08765		**HN**	HN	Barrow Hill Roundhouse, Chesterfield, Derbys (S)
08774	a	**0**	AD	AV Dawson, Ayrton Rail Terminal, Middlesbrough
08780		**G**	LS	L&NWR Heritage Company, Crewe Diesel Depot
08782	a†	**CU**	HN	Barrow Hill Roundhouse, Chesterfield, Derbys (S)

08783		E	EY	RSS, Rye Farm, Wishaw, Sutton Coldfield
08784		DG	PO	Nottingham Heritage Railway, Ruddington
08785	* a	FG	FL	Freightliner, Southampton Maritime FLT
08786	a	DG	HN	Barrow Hill Roundhouse, Chesterfield, Derbys (S)
08787		B	MR	Hunslet Engine Company, Barton-under-Needwood, Staffs (S)
08788	*	RL	RL	PD Ports, Teesport, Grangetown, Middlesbrough
08790	*	B	AM	Alstom, Longsight Depot, Manchester
08795		K	LL	Chrysalis Rail, Landore Depot, Swansea
08798		E	HN	Barrow Hill Roundhouse, Chesterfield, Derbys (S)
08799	a	HN	HN	HNRC, Worksop Depot, Nottinghamshire
08802	†	E	HN	HNRC, Worksop Depot, Nottinghamshire (S)
08804	†	E	HN	East Kent Light Railway, Shepherdswell, Kent (S)
08805		FO	WM	West Midlands Trains, Soho Depot, Birmingham
08809		RL	RL	Hanson Cement, Ketton Cement Works, nr Stamford
08810	a	LW	AV	Arriva TrainCare, Eastleigh Depot, Hampshire
08818		GB	HN	HNRC, Worksop Depot, Nottinghamshire
08822	*	IC	GW	Great Western Railway, St Philip's Marsh Depot, Bristol
08823	a	HU	ED	Tata Steel, Shotton Works, Deeside
08824	ak	K	HN	Barrow Hill Roundhouse, Chesterfield, Derbys (S)
08825		N	PO	Chinnor & Princes Risborough Railway
08834		HN	HN	Northern, Allerton Depot, Liverpool
08836	*	GW	GW	Great Western Railway, Laira Depot, Plymouth
08846		B	RS	West Midlands Trains, Tyseley Depot, Birmingham
08847	*	CD	RL	PD Ports, Teesport, Grangetown, Middlesbrough
08850	*	B	NY	North Yorkshire Moors Railway, Grosmont Depot
08853	* a	WA	ED	Wabtec Rail, Doncaster Works
08865		E	HN	HNRC, Worksop Depot, Nottinghamshire
08868		AW	HN	Arriva TrainCare, Crewe Depot, Cheshire
08870		IC	ER	Eastern Rail Services, Great Yarmouth, Norfolk
08871		CD	RL	LORAM, Derby
08872		E	HN	European Metal Recycling, Attercliffe, Sheffield (S)
08874	*	SL	RL	Weardale Railway, Wolsingham, County Durham
08877		DG	HN	HNRC, Worksop Depot, Nottinghamshire
08879		E	HN	Breedon, Hope Cement Works, Derbys (S)
08885		B	RL	Weardale Railway, Wolsingham, County Durham (S)
08887	* a	B	AM	Alstom, Wembley Depot, London
08891	*	FG	FL	Freightliner, Ipswich Depot
08892		DR	HN	HNRC, Worksop Depot, Nottinghamshire
08899		O	RS	Nemesis Rail, Burton-on-Trent, Staffordshire
08903		B	SU	SembCorp Utilities UK, Wilton, Middlesbrough
08904	d	E	HN	HNRC, Worksop Depot, Nottinghamshire (S)
08905		E	HN	Shackerstone, Battlefield Line (S)
08908		ST	EM	Northern, Neville Hill Depot, Leeds (S)
08912		B	AD	AV Dawson, Ayrton Rail Terminal, Middlesbrough (S)
08918		DG	HN	Nemesis Rail, Burton-on-Trent, Staffordshire (S)
08921		E	RS	RSS, Rye Farm, Wishaw, Sutton Coldfield (S)
08922		DG	PO	Spa Valley Railway
08924	†	GB	HN	Celsa Steel UK, Tremorfa Steelworks, Cardiff
08925		G	GB	HNRC, Worksop Depot, Nottinghamshire (S)
08927		G	RS	Avon Valley Railway
08933		B	MR	Hunslet Engine Company, Barton-under-Needwood, Staffs

08934	a	G	GB	HNRC, Worksop Depot, Nottinghamshire
08936		B	RL	Weardale Railway, Wolsingham, County Durham
08937		G	BD	Dartmoor Railway, Meldon Quarry, nr Okehampton
08939		ECR	RS	RSS, Rye Farm, Wishaw, Sutton Coldfield
08943		HN	HN	Alstom, Central Rivers Depot, Barton-under-Needwood
08947		B	MR	Hanson Aggregates, Whatley Quarry, near Frome
08948	c	EP	EU	Eurostar, Temple Mills Depot, London
08950		ST	EM	Northern, Neville Hill Depot, Leeds
08954	*	B	AM	Alstom, Polmadie Depot, Glasgow
08956		0	LO	Barrow Hill Roundhouse, Chesterfield, Derbys (S)

Other numbers or names carried:

08308	"23"		08735	Geoff Hobbs 42
08423	"LOCO 2" / "14"		08737	D3905
08442	"0042"		08743	Bryan Turner
08451	Loopy Lou		08754	"H041"
08460	SPIRIT OF THE OAK		08757	EAGLE C.U.R.C.
08483	Bungle		08762	"H067"
08484	CAPTAIN NATHANIEL DARELL		08774	ARTHUR VERNON DAWSON
08499	REDLIGHT		08780	Zippy / D3948
08525	DUNCAN BEDFORD		08787	"08296"
08567	John Atkinson Stevens		08790	LONGSIGHT TMD
	20th May 1925–19th July 1984		08799	Ian Goddard 1938–2016
08568	St. Rollox		08805	Robin Jones
08585	Vicky			40 YEARS SERVICE
08588	"H047"		08809	"24"
08602	"004"		08810	RICHARD J. WENHAM
08605	"WIGAN 2"			EASTLEIGH DEPOT
08613	"H064"			DECEMBER 1989 – JULY 1999
08615	UNCLE DAI		08818	MOLLY / "4"
08616	TYSELEY 100 / Bam Bam / 3783		08822	Dave Mills
08617	Steve Purser		08823	KEVLA
08622	"H028" / "19"		08824	"IEMD 01"
08624	Rambo PAUL RAMSEY		08846	"003"
08630	"CELSA 3"		08847	"LOCO 1"
08641	Pride of Laira		08865	GILLY
08644	Laira Diesel Depot		08871	"H074"
	50 Years 1962–2012		08885	"H042" / "18"
08645	St. Piran		08899	Midland Counties Railway
08649	Bradwell			175 1839–2014
08669	Bob Machin		08903	John W Antill
08678	"555"		08924	"CELSA 2"
08690	DAVID THIRKILL		08927	D4157
08691	Terri		08934	D4164
08703	Steve Blick (Concrete Bob)		08937	D4167
	ShunterSpot		08950	DAVID LIGHTFOOT

CLASS 09   BR/ENGLISH ELECTRIC   0-6-0

Built: 1959–62 by BR at Darlington or Horwich Works.
Engine: English Electric 6KT of 298 kW (400 hp) at 680 rpm.
Main Generator: English Electric 801.
Traction Motors: English Electric 506.
Maximum Tractive Effort: 111 kN (25000 lbf).
Continuous Tractive Effort: 39 kN (8800 lbf) at 11.6 mph.

Power at Rail: 201 kW (269 hp).	**Train Brakes:** Air & vacuum.
Brake Force: 19 t.	**Dimensions:** 8.92 x 2.59 m.
Weight: 49 t.	**Wheel Diameter:** 1372 mm.
Design Speed: 27 mph.	**Maximum Speed:** 27 mph.
Fuel Capacity: 3037 litres.	**Route Availability:** 5.
Train Supply: Not equipped.	**Total:** 10.

Class 09/0. Built as Class 09.

09002	**G**	GB	Barrow Hill Roundhouse, Chesterfield, Derbys (S)
09006	**E**	HN	Nemesis Rail, Burton-on-Trent, Staffordshire (S)
09007	**G**	LN	London Overground, Willesden Depot, London
09009	**G**	GB	RSS, Rye Farm, Wishaw, Sutton Coldfield
09014	**DG**	HN	Nemesis Rail, Burton-on-Trent, Staffordshire (S)
09022	**B**	VG	Victoria Group, Port of Boston, Boston
09023	**E**	EY	European Metal Recycling, Attercliffe, Sheffield (S)

Class 09/1. Converted from Class 08 1992–93 by RFS Industries, Kilnhurst.
110 V electrical equipment.

09106	**HN**	HN	Celsa Steel UK, Tremorfa Steelworks, Cardiff

Class 09/2. Converted from Class 08 1992 by RFS Industries, Kilnhurst.
90 V electrical equipment.

09201	**DG**	HN	HNRC, Worksop Depot, Nottinghamshire (S)
09204	**AW**	AV	Arriva TrainCare, Crewe Depot, Cheshire

Other numbers or names carried:

09007	D3671	09106	"6"
09022	PB144		

CLASS 18   CLAYTON HYBRID+   Bo-Bo

Beacon Rail ordered 15 Class 18 Bo-Bo diesel-battery hybrid shunters (Type CBD90) from Clayton Equipment as potential replacements for Classes 08/09. Although GB Railfreight hired 18001 for shunting at Whitemoor Yard at March for assessment purposes no other customers have yet been found for these locomotives which are stored awaiting developments at Wolverton.
Built: 2021–23 by Clayton Equipment Company, Burton-on-Trent.
Batteries/Engine: 524 kWh battery + JCB Dieselmax 430 of 55 kW (74 hp).
Main Generator:
Traction Motors:
Maximum Tractive Effort: 303 kN (68000 lbf).

Continuous Tractive Effort:
Power at Rail: 416 kW (558 hp).
Brake Force:
Weight: 90 t.
Design Speed: 12 mph.
Fuel Capacity:
Train Supply: Not equipped.

Train Brakes: Air.
Dimensions: 13.64 x ?? m.
Wheel Diameter:
Maximum Speed: 12 mph.
Route Availability:
Total: 15.

18001	**BN**	BN	Gemini Rail Group, Wolverton Works (S)
18002	**BN**	BN	Gemini Rail Group, Wolverton Works (S)
18003	**BN**	BN	Gemini Rail Group, Wolverton Works (S)
18004	**BN**	BN	Gemini Rail Group, Wolverton Works (S)
18005	**BN**	BN	Gemini Rail Group, Wolverton Works (S)
18006	**BN**	BN	Gemini Rail Group, Wolverton Works (S)
18007	**BN**	BN	Gemini Rail Group, Wolverton Works (S)
18008	**BN**	BN	Gemini Rail Group, Wolverton Works (S)
18009	**BN**	BN	Gemini Rail Group, Wolverton Works (S)
18010	**BN**	BN	Gemini Rail Group, Wolverton Works (S)
18011	**BN**	BN	Gemini Rail Group, Wolverton Works (S)
18012	**BN**	BN	Gemini Rail Group, Wolverton Works (S)
18013	**BN**	BN	Gemini Rail Group, Wolverton Works (S)
18014	**BN**	BN	Gemini Rail Group, Wolverton Works (S)
18015	**BN**	BN	Gemini Rail Group, Wolverton Works (S)

1.2. MAIN LINE DIESEL LOCOMOTIVES

CLASS 20   ENGLISH ELECTRIC   Bo-Bo

Built: 1957–68 by English Electric at Vulcan Foundry, Newton-le-Willows or by Robert Stephenson & Hawthorns at Darlington.
Engine: English Electric 8SVT Mk II of 746 kW (1000 hp) at 850 rpm.
Main Generator: English Electric 819/3C.
Traction Motors: English Electric 526/5D or 526/8D.
Maximum Tractive Effort: 187 kN (42000 lbf).
Continuous Tractive Effort: 111 kN (25000 lbf) at 11 mph.
Power at Rail: 574 kW (770 hp).
Brake Force: 35 t.
Weight: 73.4–73.5 t.
Design Speed: 75 mph.
Fuel Capacity: 1727 litres.
Train Supply: Not equipped.

Train Brakes: Air & vacuum.
Dimensions: 14.25 x 2.67 m.
Wheel Diameter: 1092 mm.
Maximum Speed: 75 mph.
Route Availability: 5.
Total: 28.

Non-standard liveries/numbering:

20056	Yellow with grey cabsides and red solebar. Carries No. "81".
20066	Dark blue with yellow stripes. Carries No. "82".
20096	Carries original number D8096.
20107	Carries original number D8107.
20110	Carries original number D8110.
20142	LUL Maroon.

20168 Breedon Aggregates. Carries No. "2".
20227 LUL Maroon.
20906 White. Carries No. "3".

Class 20/0. Standard Design.

20007	**G**	EE	MOLO	SK	
20056	**O**	HN	HNRL	SC (S)	
20066	**O**	HN	HNRL	BH (S)	
20096	**G**	LS	LSLO	CL	
20107	**G**	LS	LSLO	CL	Jocelyn Feilding 1940–2020
20118	**FO**	LS	LSLO	CL	Saltburn-by-the-Sea
20121	**HN**	HN	HNRL	BH (S)	
20132	**FO**	LS	LSLO	CL	
20142	**O**	20	MOLO	SK	SIR JOHN BETJEMAN
20168	**O**	HN	HNRL	BH	SIR GEORGE EARLE
20189	**B**	20	MOLO	SK	
20205	**B**	2L	MOLO	SK	
20227	**O**	2L	MOLO	SK	SHERLOCK HOLMES

Class 20/3. Locomotives refurbished by Direct Rail Services in the 1990s.
Details as Class 20/0 except:

Refurbished: 15 locomotives were refurbished 1995–96 by Brush Traction at Loughborough (20301–305) or 1997–98 by RFS(E) at Doncaster (20306–315). Disc indicators or headcode panels removed.
Train Brakes: Air.   **Maximum Speed:** 60 mph (+ 75 mph).
Weight: 73 t (+ 76 t).   **Fuel Capacity:** 2909 (+ 4909) litres.
Brake Force: 35 t (+ 31 t).   **RA:** 5 (+ 6).

20301	(20047)	r	**DS**	HN	HNRS	BH (S)
20302	(20084)	r	**DS**	HN	HNRS	BH (S)
20303	(20127)	r	**DS**	HN	HNRS	WS (S)
20304	(20120)	r	**DS**	HN	HNRS	WS (S)
20305	(20095)	r	**DS**	HN	HNRS	BQ (S)
20308	(20187)	r+	**DS**	HN	HNRS	WS (S)
20309	(20075)	r+	**DS**	HN	HNRS	HO
20311	(20102)	r+	**HN**	HN	HNRL	BH (S)
20312	(20042)	r+	**DS**	HN	HNRS	WS (S)
20314	(20117)	r+	**HN**	HN	HNRL	WS

Class 20/9. Harry Needle Railroad Company (former Hunslet-Barclay/DRS) locomotives. Details as Class 20/0 except:

Refurbished: 1989 by Hunslet-Barclay at Kilmarnock.
Train Brakes: Air.   **Fuel Capacity:** 1727 (+ 4727) litres.
RA: 5 (+ 6).

20901	(20101)		**GB**	HN	HNRL	WS
20903	(20083)	+	**DR**	HN	HNRS	BU (S)
20904	(20041)		**DR**	HN	HNRS	BU (S)
20905	(20225)	+	**GB**	HN	HNRL	WS
20906	(20219)		**O**	HN	HNRL	HO

CLASS 25　BR/BEYER PEACOCK/SULZER　Bo-Bo

Built: 1965 by Beyer Peacock at Gorton.
Engine: Sulzer 6LDA28-B of 930 kW (1250 hp) at 750 rpm.
Main Generator: AEI RTB15656.　**Traction Motors:** AEI 253AY.
Maximum Tractive Effort: 200 kN (45000 lbf).
Continuous Tractive Effort: 93 kN (20800 lbf) at 17.1 mph.
Power at Rail: 708 kW (949 hp).　**Train Brakes:** Air & vacuum.
Brake Force: 38 t.　**Dimensions:** 15.39 x 2.73 m.
Weight: 71.5 t.　**Wheel Diameter:** 1143 mm.
Design Speed: 90 mph.　**Maximum Speed:** 60 mph.
Fuel Capacity: 2270 litres.　**Route Availability:** 5.
Train Supply: Not equipped.　**Total:** 1.

Carries original number D7628.

Only certified for use on Network Rail tracks between Whitby and Grosmont, as an extension of North Yorkshire Moors Railway services.

25278	**GG**	NY	MBDL	NY	SYBILLA

CLASS 31　BRUSH/ENGLISH ELECTRIC　A1A-A1A

Built: 1958–62 by Brush Traction at Loughborough.
Engine: English Electric 12SVT of 1100 kW (1470 hp) at 850 rpm.
Main Generator: Brush TG160-48.　**Traction Motors:** Brush TM73-68.
Maximum Tractive Effort: 160 kN (35900 lbf).
Continuous Tractive Effort: 83 kN (18700 lbf) at 23.5 mph.
Power at Rail: 872 kW (1170 hp).　**Train Brakes:** Air & vacuum.
Brake Force: 49 t.　**Dimensions:** 17.30 x 2.67 m.
Weight: 106.7–111 t.　**Wheel Diameter:** 1092/1003 mm.
Design Speed: 90 mph.　**Maximum Speed:** 90 mph.
Fuel Capacity: 2409 litres.　**Route Availability:** 5.
Train Supply: Not equipped.　**Total:** 3.

Non-standard livery: 31452 All over dark green.

31106	**B**	HH		BU (S)	
31128	**B**	NS	NRLO	BU	CHARYBDIS
31452	**0**	ER	ERSL	YA	

CLASS 33　BRCW/SULZER　Bo-Bo

Built: 1959–62 by the Birmingham Railway Carriage & Wagon Company at Smethwick.
Engine: Sulzer 8LDA28 of 1160 kW (1550 hp) at 750 rpm.
Main Generator: Crompton Parkinson CG391B1.
Traction Motors: Crompton Parkinson C171C2.
Maximum Tractive Effort: 200 kN (45000 lbf).
Continuous Tractive Effort: 116 kN (26000 lbf) at 17.5 mph.
Power at Rail: 906 kW (1215 hp).　**Train Brakes:** Air & vacuum.
Brake Force: 35 t.　**Dimensions:** 15.47 x 2.82 (2.64 m 33/2).

Weight: 76-78 t.
Design Speed: 85 mph.
Fuel Capacity: 3410 litres.
Train Supply: Electric, index 48 (750 V DC only).
Total: 5.

Wheel Diameter: 1092 mm.
Maximum Speed: 85 mph.
Route Availability: 6.

Non-standard numbering: 33012 Carries original number D6515.

Class 33/0. Standard Design.

33012	**G**	71	MBDL	SW	Lt Jenny Lewis RN
33025	**WC**	WC	AWCA	CS	
33029	**WC**	WC	AWCX	CS	
33030	**DR**	WC	AWCX	CS (S)	

Class 33/2. Built to former Loading Gauge of Tonbridge–Battle Line.
Equipped with slow speed control.

33207	**WC**	WC	AWCA	CS	Jim Martin

CLASS 37   ENGLISH ELECTRIC   Co-Co

Built: 1960–66 by English Electric at Vulcan Foundry, Newton-le-Willows or by Robert Stephenson & Hawthorns at Darlington.
Engine: English Electric 12CSVT of 1300 kW (1750 hp) at 850 rpm.
Main Generator: English Electric 822/10G.
Traction Motors: English Electric 538/A.
Maximum Tractive Effort: 247 kN (55500 lbf).
Continuous Tractive Effort: 156 kN (35000 lbf) at 13.6 mph.
Power at Rail: 932 kW (1250 hp).   **Train Brakes:** Air & vacuum.
Brake Force: 50 t.   **Dimensions:** 18.75 x 2.74 m.
Weight: 102.8–108.4 t.   **Wheel Diameter:** 1092 mm.
Design Speed: 90 mph.   **Maximum Speed:** 80 mph.
Fuel Capacity: 4046 (+ 7683) litres.   **Route Availability:** 5.
Train Supply: Not equipped.   **Total:** 62.

Non-standard liveries and numbering:

37424 Also carries the number 37558.
37508 Previously numbered 37606.
37521 Carries original number D6817.
37667 Carries original number D6851.
37688 Two-tone trainload freight grey with Construction decals.
37703 Carries the number 37067.
37905 Also carries original number D6836.

Class 37/0. Standard Design.

37025	**BL**	37	COTS	BO (S)	Inverness TMD
37038 a	**DI**	HN	HNRS	WS (S)	
37057	**CS**	CS	COTS	NM	Barbara Arbon
37059 ar+	**DI**	HN	HNRS	BQ (S)	
37069 ar+	**DI**	DR	XSDP	CR (S)	
37099	**CS**	CS	COTS	NM	MERL EVANS 1947–2016
37116 +	**CS**	CS	COTS	NM	

37175 a	**CS**	CS	COTS	NM	
37190	**B**	LS	MBDL	MG (S)	
37207	**B**	EP	EPUK	GCR (S)	
37218 ar+	**DR**	DR	XHSO	KM	
37219	**CS**	CS	COTS	NM	Jonty Jarvis 8-12-1998 to 18-3-2005
37240	**F**	VT	MBDL	NM	
37254	**CS**	CS	COTS	NM	Cardiff Canton
37259 ar	**DS**	HN	HNRS	WS (S)	

Class 37/4. Refurbished with electric train supply equipment. Main generator replaced by alternator. Regeared (CP7) bogies. Details as Class 37/0 except:
Main Alternator: Brush BA1005A.   **Power At Rail:** 935 kW (1254 hp).
Traction Motors: English Electric 538/5A.
Maximum Tractive Effort: 256 kN (57440 lbf).
Continuous Tractive Effort: 184 kN (41250 lbf) at 11.4 mph.
Weight: 107 t.   **Design Speed:** 80 mph.
Fuel Capacity: 7683 litres.
Train Supply: Electric, index 30.

37401 ar	**BL**	DR	XHSO	KM	Mary Queen of Scots
37402 a	**BL**	DR	XSDP	CR (S)	
37403	**BL**	SP	RAJV	NY	Isle of Mull
37405 ar	**HN**	HN	COFS	BH	
37407	**BL**	DR	XHSO	KM	Blackpool Tower
37409 ar	**BL**	LS	LSLO	BH (S)	Lord Hinton
37418	**BL**	SB	LRLO	NM	An Comunn Gaidhealach
37419 ar	**IC**	DR	XHSO	KM	Driver Tony Kay 1974–2019
37421	**CS**	CS	COTS	NM	
37422 ar	**DR**	DR	XHSO	KM	Victorious
37423 ar	**DR**	DR	XSDP	CR (S)	Spirit of the Lakes
37424	**BL**	DR	XHSO	KM	Avro Vulcan XH558
37425 ar	**RR**	DR	XHSO	KM	Sir Robert McAlpine/Concrete Bob

Class 37/5. Refurbished without train supply equipment. Main generator replaced by alternator. Regeared (CP7) bogies. Details as Class 37/4 except:
Power At Rail: 932 kW (1250 hp).
Maximum Tractive Effort: 248 kN (55590 lbf).
Weight: 106.1–110.0 t.
Train Supply: Not equipped.

37508	**FO**	SB	LRLO	BU (S)	
37510 a	**EX**	EP	GROG	LR	Orion
37516 s	**WC**	WC	AWCA	CS	Loch Laidon
37517 as	**LH**	WC	AWCX	CS (S)	
37518 ar	**WC**	WC	AWCA	CS	Fort William/An Gearasdan
37521	**G**	LS	LSLO	CL	

Class 37/6. Originally refurbished for Nightstar services. Main generator replaced by alternator. UIC jumpers. Details as Class 37/5 except:
Maximum Speed: 90 mph.   **Train Brake:** Air.
Train Supply: Not equipped, but electric through wired.

37601 ad	**EX**	EP	GROG	LR	Perseus

37602	ar	**DS**	HN	HNRS	BH (S)	
37603	a	**DS**	HN	HNRL	WS (S)	
37604	a	**DS**	HN	HNRL	WS (S)	
37607	ar	**HN**	HN	COTS	BH	
37608	ard	**EX**	EP	GROG	LR	Andromeda
37609	a	**DI**	EP	HNRL	WS (S)	
37610	ar	**BL**	HN	COTS	BH	
37611	ad	**RO**	EP	GROG	LR	Denise
37612	a	**DR**	HN	COTS	BH	

Class 37/5 continued.

37667	ars	**G**	LS	LSLO	CL	FLOPSIE
37668	e	**WC**	WC	AWCA	CS	
37669	e	**WC**	WC	AWCA	CS	
37676	a	**WC**	WC	AWCA	CS	Loch Rannoch
37685	a	**WC**	WC	AWCA	CS	Loch Arkaig
37688		**0**	D0	MBDL	CL	Great Rocks

Class 37/7. Refurbished locomotives. Main generator replaced by alternator. Regeared (CP7) bogies. Ballast weights added. Details as Class 37/5 except:
Main Alternator: GEC G564AZ (37800) Brush BA1005A (others).
Maximum Tractive Effort: 276 kN (62000 lbf).
Weight: 120 t.   **Route Availability:** 7.

37706		**WC**	WC	AWCA	CS	
37712	a	**WC**	WC	AWCX	CS (S)	
37716		**DI**	DR	XHSO	KM	
37800	d	**RO**	EP	GROG	LR	
37884	d	**EX**	EP	GROG	LR	Cepheus

Class 37/9. Refurbished locomotives. New power unit. Main generator replaced by alternator. Ballast weights added. Details as Class 37/4 except:
Engine: * Mirrlees 6MB275T of 1340 kW (1800 hp) or † Ruston 6RK270T of 1340 kW (1800 hp) at 900 rpm.
Main Alternator: Brush BA15005A.
Maximum Tractive Effort: 279 kN (62680 lbf).
Weight: 120 t.   **Route Availability:** 7.
Train Supply: Not equipped.

37901	*	**EX**	EP	EPUK	LR	Mirrlees Pioneer
37905	†	**G**	UR	UKRM	LR (S)	
37906	†	**FO**	UR	UKRM	BL (S)	

Class 97/3. Class 37s refurbished for use on the Cambrian Lines which are signalled by ERTMS. Details as Class 37/0.

97301	(37100) e	**Y**	NR	QETS	RO (S)	
97302	(37170) e	**Y**	NR	QETS	ZA	Ffestiniog & Welsh Highland Railways/Rheilffyrdd Ffestiniog ac Eryri
97303	(37178) e	**Y**	NR	QETS	ZA	Dave Berry
97304	(37217) e	**Y**	NR	QETS	ZA	John Tiley

CLASS 40   ENGLISH ELECTRIC   1Co-Co1

Built: 1961 by English Electric at Vulcan Foundry, Newton-le-Willows.
Engine: English Electric 16SVT Mk2 of 1492 kW (2000 hp) at 850 rpm.
Main Generator: English Electric 822/4C.
Traction Motors: English Electric 526/5D or EE526/7D.
Maximum Tractive Effort: 231 kN (52000 lbf).
Continuous Tractive Effort: 137 kN (30900 lbf) at 18.8 mph.

Power at Rail: 1160 kW (1550 hp).   **Train Brakes:** Air & vacuum.
Brake Force: 51 t.   **Dimensions:** 21.18 x 2.78 m.
Weight: 132 t.   **Wheel Diameter:** 914/1143 mm.
Design Speed: 90 mph.   **Maximum Speed:** 90 mph.
Fuel Capacity: 3250 litres.   **Route Availability:** 6.
Train Supply: Steam heating.   **Total:** 2.

40013 Carries original number D213.
40145 Carries original number 345.

40013	**G**	ST	LSLO	CL	Andania
40145	**G**	40	CFSL	CS	

CLASS 43   BREL/PAXMAN   Bo-Bo

Built: 1975–82 by BREL at Crewe Works.
Engine: MTU 16V4000 R41R of 1680kW (2250 hp) at 1500 rpm.
(* Paxman 12VP185 of 1680 kW (2250 hp) at 1500 rpm.)
Main Alternator: Brush BA1001B.
Traction Motors: Brush TMH68–46 or GEC G417AZ (43124–152); frame mounted.
Maximum Tractive Effort: 80 kN (17980 lbf).
Continuous Tractive Effort: 46 kN (10340 lbf) at 64.5 mph.

Power at Rail: 1320 kW (1770 hp).   **Train Brakes:** Air.
Brake Force: 35 t.   **Dimensions:** 17.79 x 2.74 m.
Weight: 70.25–75.0 t.   **Wheel Diameter:** 1020 mm.
Design Speed: 125 mph.   **Maximum Speed:** 125 mph.
Fuel Capacity: 4500 litres.   **Route Availability:** 5.
Train Supply: Three-phase electric.   **Total:** 159.

† Buffer fitted.
§ Modified GWR power cars that can operate with power door fitted short sets.

43013, 43014 & 43062 are fitted with measuring apparatus & front-end cameras.

43184 regained its original number in 2022, having been renumbered back from 43384.

43008, 43009, 43010, 43016, 43040, 43172, 43184, 43192, 43239, 43304, 43366 are due to be exported.

Non-standard liveries:

43007 Original HST blue & yellow.
43206 Original HST blue & yellow. Carries the number 43006
43238 All-over red
43312 Original HST blue & yellow. Carries the number 43112

43003		**SI**	A	HAPC	HA
43004	§	**GW**	A	EFPC	LA	Caerphilly Castle
43007		**O**	A	EFPC	EP (S)
43008		**IC**	A	EFPC	YA (S)
43009	§	**GW**	GW	EFPC	YA (S)
43010	§	**GW**	GW	SCEL	YA (S)
43012		**SI**	A	HAPC	HA
43013	†	**Y**	P	QCAR	ZA	Mark Carne CBE
43014	†	**Y**	P	QCAR	ZA
43015		**SI**	A	HAPC	HA
43016	§	**GW**	A	EFPC	YA (S)
43017		**FB**	A	SCEL	EP (S)
43020		**FB**	A	SCEL	EP (S)	MTU Power. Passion. Partnership
43021		**SI**	A	HAPC	HA
43023		**FB**	A	SCEL	EP (S)
43024		**FB**	A	SCEL	EP (S)
43025		**FB**	125	ICHP	EP (S)
43026		**SI**	A	HAPC	HA
43027	§	**GW**	GW	EFPC	LA	Acton Castle
43028		**SI**	A	HAPC	HA
43029	§	**GW**	GW	EFPC	LA	Caldicot Castle
43030		**SI**	A	HAPC	ZK (S)
43031		**SI**	A	HAPC	HA
43032		**SI**	A	HAPC	HA
43033		**SI**	A	HAPC	HA
43034		**SI**	A	HAPC	HA
43035		**SI**	A	HAPC	HA
43036		**SI**	A	HAPC	HA
43037		**SI**	A	HAPC	HA
43040	§	**GW**	A	EFPC	YA (S)
43042	§	**GW**	A	EFPC	LA	Tregenna Castle
43044	*	**IE**	125	ICHP	RD	Edward Paxman
43046	*	**MP**	LS	LSLO	CL	Geoff Drury 1930–1999 Steam Preservation and Computerised Track Recording Pioneer
43047	*	**MP**	LS	LSLO	CL
43048	*	**ST**	125	ICHP	RD
43049	*	**IC**	LS	LSLO	CL	Neville Hill
43050	*	**ST**	P	SBXL	LB
43054	*	**ST**	DA	MBDL	LB
43055	*	**MP**	LS	LSLO	CL
43058	*	**RC**	LS	LSLO	CL
43059	*	**MP**	LS	LSLO	CL
43062		**Y**	P	QCAR	ZA	John Armitt
43063		**FB**	GW	SBXL	LA (S)

43066 *	**ST**	DA	MBDL	LB	
43076 *	**ST**	DA	MBDL	LB	
43083 *	**ST**	LS	LSLO	ZG (S)	
43088 §	**GW**	FG	EFPC	LA (S)	
43089 *	**ST**	125	ICHP	RD	
43091	**FB**	GW	SBXL	LA (S)	
43092 §	**GW**	FG	EFPC	LA	Cromwell's Castle
43093 §	**GW**	FG	EFPC	LA	Berkeley Castle
43094 §	**GW**	FG	EFPC	LA	St Mawes Castle
43097 §	**GW**	FG	EFPC	LA	Castle Drogo
43098 §	**GW**	FG	EFPC	LA	Walton Castle
43122 §	**GW**	FG	EFPC	LA	Dunster Castle
43124	**SI**	A	HAPC	HA	
43125	**SI**	A	HAPC	HA	
43126	**SI**	A	HAPC	HA	
43127	**SI**	A	HAPC	HA	
43128	**SI**	A	HAPC	HA	
43129	**SI**	A	HAPC	HA	
43130	**SI**	A	HAPC	HA	
43131	**SI**	A	HAPC	HA	
43132	**SI**	A	HAPC	HA	
43133	**SI**	A	HAPC	HA	
43134	**SI**	A	HAPC	HA	Gordon Aikman BEM MND Campaigner 1985–2017
43135	**SI**	A	HAPC	HA	
43136	**SI**	A	HAPC	HA	
43137	**SI**	A	HAPC	HA	
43138	**SI**	A	HAPC	HA	
43139	**SI**	A	HAPC	HA	
43141	**SI**	A	HAPC	HA	
43142	**SI**	A	HAPC	HA	
43143	**SI**	A	HAPC	HA	
43144	**SI**	A	HAPC	HA	
43145	**SI**	A	HAPC	HA	
43146	**SI**	A	HAPC	HA	
43147	**SI**	A	HAPC	HA	
43148	**SI**	A	HAPC	HA	
43149	**SI**	A	HAPC	HA	
43150	**SI**	A	HAPC	HA	
43151	**SI**	A	HAPC	HA	
43152	**SI**	A	HAPC	HA	
43153 §	**GW**	FG	EFPC	LA	Chûn Castle
43154 §	**GW**	FG	EFPC	LA	Compton Castle
43155 §	**GW**	FG	EFPC	LA	Rougemont Castle
43156 §	**GW**	FG	EFPC	LA	Maen Castle
43159	**FB**	125	ICHP	RD	
43160 §	**GW**	FG	EFPC	LA (S)	
43161	**FB**	GW	SBXL	LA (S)	
43162 §	**GW**	FG	EFPC	LA	Caerhays Castle
43163	**SI**	A	HAPC	HA	
43164	**SI**	A	HAPC	HA	

43165	**FB**	A	SCEL	EP (S)	
43168	**SI**	A	HAPC	HA	
43169	**SI**	A	HAPC	HA	
43172 §	**GW**	GW	EFPC	YA (S)	
43174	**FB**	A	SCEL	EP (S)	
43175	**SI**	A	HAPC	HA	
43176	**SI**	A	HAPC	HA	
43177	**SI**	A	HAPC	HA	
43179	**SI**	A	HAPC	HA	
43181	**SI**	A	HAPC	HA	
43182	**SI**	A	HAPC	HA	
43183	**SI**	A	HAPC	HA	
43184	**IE**	A	EHPC	YA (S)	
43185	**IC**	A	SCEL	ZK (S)	
43186 §	**GW**	A	EFPC	LA	Taunton Castle
43187 §	**GW**	A	EFPC	LA	Cardiff Castle
43188 §	**GW**	A	EFPC	LA	Newport Castle
43189 §	**GW**	A	EFPC	LA	Launceston Castle
43190	**FB**	A	SCEL	EP (S)	
43191	**FB**	A	SCEL	EP (S)	
43192 §	**GW**	A	SCEL	YA (S)	
43194 §	**GW**	FG	EFPC	LA	Okehampton Castle
43198 §	**GW**	FG	EFPC	LA	Driver Stan Martin 25 June 1950 – 6 November 2004/Driver Brian Cooper 15 June 1947 – 5 October 1999

Class 43/2. Rebuilt CrossCountry and former LNER, East Midlands Railway or Grand Central power cars. Power cars were renumbered by adding 200 to their original number or 400 to their original number (former Grand Central), except 43123 which became 43423.

43206 (43006)	**0**	A	IECP	EP (S)	
43238 (43038)	**0**	A	IECP	EP (S)	
43239 (43039)	**XC**	A	EHPC	YA (S)	
43251 (43051)	**VE**	P	COTS	ZA	
43257 (43057)	**VE**	P	COTS	ZA	
43272 (43072)	**VE**	P	COTS	ZA	
43274 (43074)	**ER**	P	COTS	ZA	
43277 (43077)	**CT**	P	COTS	ZA	Safety Task Force
43285 (43085)	**XC**	P	EHPC	ZA	
43290 (43090)	**VE**	P	COTS	ZA	
43295 (43095)	**VE**	A	SCEL	EP (S)	
43296 (43096)	**VE**	RA	HHPC	ZG (S)	
43299 (43099)	**VE**	P	COTS	ZA	
43300 (43100)	**VE**	P	IECP	Reid's, Stoke (S)	
43301 (43101)	**XC**	P	EHPC	OD (S)	
43303 (43103)	**XC**	P	EHPC	OD (S)	
43304 (43104)	**XC**	A	EHPC	YA (S)	
43305 (43105)	**VE**	A	SCEL	EP (S)	
43306 (43106)	**VE**	A	SCEL	EP (S)	
43307 (43107)	**VE**	A	SCEL	EP (S)	
43308 (43108)	**VE**	RA	HHPC	ZG (S)	

43309 (43109)	**VE**	A	SCEL	EP (S)	
43310 (43110)	**VE**	A	SCEL	EP (S)	
43311 (43111)	**VE**	A	SCEL	EP (S)	
43312 (43112)	**0**	A	SCEL	EP (S)	
43314 (43114)	**VE**	A	SCEL	EP (S)	
43315 (43115)	**VE**	A	SCEL	EP (S)	
43316 (43116)	**VE**	A	SCEL	EP (S)	
43317 (43117)	**VE**	A	SCEL	EP (S)	
43318 (43118)	**VE**	A	SCEL	EP (S)	
43319 (43119)	**VE**	A	SCEL	EP (S)	
43320 (43120)	**VE**	A	SCEL	EP (S)	
43321 (43121)	**XC**	P	EHPC	OD (S)	
43357 (43157)	**XC**	P	EHPC	OD (S)	
43366 (43166)	**XC**	A	EHPC	YA (S)	
43367 (43167)	**VE**	A	SCEL	EP (S)	
43378 (43178)	**XC**	A	EHPC	EP (S)	
43423 (43123) †	**EA**	RA	HHPC	ZG (S)	
43465 (43065) †	**RA**	RA	HHPC	KI	
43467 (43067) †	**EA**	RA	HHPC	ZG (S)	
43468 (43068) †	**RA**	RA	HHPC	KI	
43480 (43080) †	**RA**	RA	HHPC	KI	
43484 (43084) †	**RA**	RA	HHPC	KI	

CLASS 45   BR/SULZER   1Co-Co1

Built: 1963 by BR at Derby Locomotive Works.
Engine: Sulzer 12LDA28B of 1860 kW (2500 hp) at 750 rpm.
Main Generator: Crompton-Parkinson CG426 A1.
Traction Motors: Crompton-Parkinson C172 A1.
Maximum Tractive Effort: 245 kN (55000 lbf).
Continuous Tractive Effort: 134 kN (31600 lbf) at 22.3 mph.

Power at Rail: 1491 kW (2000 hp).	**Train Brakes:** Air & vacuum.
Brake Force: 63 t.	**Dimensions:** 20.70 x 2.78 m.
Weight: 135 t.	**Wheel Diameter:** 914/1143 mm.
Design Speed: 90 mph.	**Maximum Speed:** 90 mph.
Fuel Capacity: 3591 litres.	**Route Availability:** 6.
Train Supply: Electric, index 66.	**Total:** 1.

45118	**B**	LS	LSLS	BH	THE ROYAL ARTILLERYMAN	

CLASS 47   BR/BRUSH/SULZER   Co-Co

Built: 1963–67 by Brush Traction, at Loughborough or by BR at Crewe Works.
Engine: Sulzer 12LDA28C of 1920 kW (2580 hp) at 750 rpm.
Main Generator: Brush TG160-60 Mk4 or TM172-50 Mk1.
Traction Motors: Brush TM64-68 Mk1 or Mk1A.
Maximum Tractive Effort: 267 kN (60000 lbf).
Continuous Tractive Effort: 133 kN (30000 lbf) at 26 mph.
Power at Rail: 1550 kW (2080 hp).   **Train Brakes:** Air.
Brake Force: 61 t.   **Dimensions:** 19.38 x 2.79 m.
Weight: 111.5–120.6 t.   **Wheel Diameter:** 1143 mm.
Design Speed: 95 mph.   **Maximum Speed:** 95 mph.
Fuel Capacity: 3273 (+ 5887) litres.   **Route Availability:** 6 or 7.
Train Supply: Not equipped.   **Total:** 45.

Class 47s exported for use abroad are listed in section 5 of this book.

Non-standard liveries/numbering:

47270   Also carries original number 1971.
47501   Carries original number D1944.
47614   Carries original number 1733.
47739   GBRf dark blue.
47773   Also carries original number D1755.
47798   Royal Train claret with Rail Express Systems markings.
47805   Carries original number D1935.
47810   Carries original number D1924.
47830   Also carries original number D1645.

Recent renumberings:

47077 carried the number 47840 from 1989 until it entered preservation.
47593 was renumbered from 47790 in 2019.
47614 was renumbered from 47853 in 2019.

Class 47/0. Standard Design. Built with train air and vacuum brakes.

47077 +	**B**	DE	MBDL	NY	NORTH STAR
47237 x+	**WC**	WC	AWCA	CS	
47245 x+	**WC**	WC	AWCA	CS	V.E. Day 75th Anniversary
47270 +	**B**	WC	AWCA	CS	

Class 47/3. Built with train air and vacuum brakes. Details as Class 47/0 except: **Weight:** 113.7 t.

47355 a+	**K**	WC	AWCX	CS (S)	

Class 47/4. Electric Train Supply equipment.
Details as Class 47/0 except:

Weight: 120.4–125.1 t.   **Fuel Capacity:** 3273 (+ 5537) litres.
Train Supply: Electric, index 66. **Route Availability:** 7.

47501 x+	**GG**	LS	LSLO	CL	CRAFTSMAN
47526 x	**BL**	WC	AWCX	CS (S)	
47580 x	**BL**	47	MBDL	TM	County of Essex

| 47593 | **BL** | LS | LSLO | CL | Galloway Princess |
| 47614 + | **B** | LS | LSLO | CL | |

Class 47/7. Previously fitted with an older form of TDM.
Details as Class 47/4 except:

Weight: 118.7 t. **Fuel Capacity:** 5887 litres.
Maximum Speed: 100 mph.

47703	**FR**	HN	HNRL	ZB	
47712	**IC**	CD	LSLO	CL	Lady Diana Spencer
47714	**AR**	HN	HNRL	ZB	
47715	**N**	HN	HNRL	WS	

Class 47/7. Former Railnet dedicated locomotives.
Details as Class 47/0 except:

Fuel Capacity: 5887 litres.

47727	**CA**	GB	GBDF	LR	Edinburgh Castle/
					Caisteal Dhùn Èideann
47739	**0**	GB	GBDF	LR	
47746 x	**WC**	WC	AWCA	CS	Chris Fudge 29.7.70 – 22.6.10
47749 d	**B**	GB	GBDF	LR	CITY OF TRURO
47760	**WC**	WC	AWCA	CS	
47768	**RX**	WC	AWCX	CS (S)	
47772	**WC**	WC	AWCA	CS	Carnforth TMD
47773 x	**GG**	70	MBDL	TM	
47776 x	**RX**	WC	AWCX	CS (S)	
47786	**WC**	WC	AWCA	CS	Roy Castle OBE
47787	**WC**	WC	AWCX	CS (S)	

Class 47/4 continued. Route Availability: 6.

47798 x	**0**	NM	MBDL	YK	Prince William
47802 +	**WC**	WC	AWCA	CS	
47804	**WC**	WC	AWCA	CS	
47805 +	**GG**	LS	LSLO	CL	Roger Hosking MA 1925–2013
47810 +	**GG**	LS	LSLO	CL	Crewe Diesel Depot
47812 +	**WC**	WC	AWCA	CS	
47813 +	**RO**	WC	AWCA	CS	
47815 +	**GG**	WC	AWCA	CS	Great Western
47816 +	**GL**	LS	DHLT	CL (S)	
47818 +	**DS**	AF	MBDL	ZG (S)	
47826 +	**WC**	WC	AWCA	CS	
47828 +	**IC**	D0	LSLO	CL	
47830 +	**GG**	FL	DFLH	CB	BEECHING'S LEGACY
47832 +	**WC**	WC	AWCA	CS	
47841 +	**IC**	LS	LSLS	MG (S)	The Institution of Mechanical
					Engineers
47843 +	**RB**	HN	SROG	WS (S)	
47847 +	**BL**	HN	SROG	WS (S)	
47848 +	**WC**	WC	AWCA	CS	
47851 +	**WC**	WC	AWCA	CS	
47854 +	**WC**	WC	AWCA	CS	Diamond Jubilee

CLASS 50　　　ENGLISH ELECTRIC　　　Co-Co

Built: 1967–68 by English Electric at Vulcan Foundry, Newton-le-Willows.
Engine: English Electric 16CVST of 2010 kW (2700 hp) at 850 rpm.
Main Generator: English Electric 840/4B.
Traction Motors: English Electric 538/5A.
Maximum Tractive Effort: 216 kN (48500 lbf).
Continuous Tractive Effort: 147 kN (33000 lbf) at 23.5 mph.
Power at Rail: 1540 kW (2070 hp).　　**Train Brakes:** Air & vacuum.
Brake Force: 59 t.　　　　　　　　　**Dimensions:** 20.88 x 2.78 m.
Weight: 116.9 t.　　　　　　　　　　**Wheel Diameter:** 1092 mm.
Design Speed: 105 mph.　　　　　　**Maximum Speed:** 90 mph.
Fuel Capacity: 4796 litres.　　　　　**Route Availability:** 6.
Train Supply: Electric, index 61.　　　**Total:** 5.

Non-standard numbering:

50007　Running with the number 50014 and "Warspite" name on one side.
50050　Also carries original number D400.

50007	**GB**	50	CFOL	KR	Hercules
50008	**HH**	HH	HVAC	BH	Thunderer
50044	**B**	50	CFOL	KR	Exeter
50049	**GB**	50	CFOL	KR	Defiance
50050	**B**	NB	COFS	NM	Fearless

CLASS 52　　　BR/MAYBACH　　　C-C

Built: 1961–64 by BR at Swindon Works.
Engine: Two Maybach MD655 of 1007 kW (1350 hp) each at 1500 rpm.
Transmission: Hydraulic. Voith L630rV.
Maximum Tractive Effort: 297 kN (66700 lbf).
Continuous Tractive Effort: 201 kN (45200 lbf) at 14.5 mph.
Power at Rail: 1490 kW (2000 hp).　　**Train Brakes:** Air & vacuum.
Brake Force: 83 t.　　　　　　　　　**Dimensions:** 20.70 m x 2.78 m.
Weight: 110 t.　　　　　　　　　　　**Wheel Diameter:** 1092 mm.
Design Speed: 90 mph.　　　　　　　**Maximum Speed:** 90 mph.
Fuel Capacity: 3900 litres.　　　　　**Route Availability:** 6.
Train Supply: Steam heating.　　　　**Total:** 1.

Never allocated a number in the 1972 number series.

D1015	**B**	DT	MBDL	KR	WESTERN CHAMPION

CLASS 55   ENGLISH ELECTRIC   Co-Co

Built: 1961 by English Electric at Vulcan Foundry, Newton-le-Willows.
Engine: Two Napier-Deltic D18-25 of 1230 kW (1650 hp) each at 1500 rpm.
Main Generators: Two English Electric 829/1A.
Traction Motors: English Electric 538/A.
Maximum Tractive Effort: 222 kN (50000 lbf).
Continuous Tractive Effort: 136 kN (30500 lbf) at 32.5 mph.
Power at Rail: 1969 kW (2640 hp).   **Train Brakes:** Air & vacuum.
Brake Force: 51 t.   **Dimensions:** 21.18 x 2.68 m.
Weight: 100 t.   **Wheel Diameter:** 1092 mm.
Design Speed: 105 mph.   **Maximum Speed:** 100 mph.
Fuel Capacity: 3755 litres.   **Route Availability:** 5.
Train Supply: Electric, index 66.   **Total:** 4.

Non-standard numbering:

55002	Carries original number D9002.	
55009	Carries original number D9009.	
55016	Carries original number D9016.	

55002	**GG**	NM	MBDL	YK		THE KING'S OWN YORKSHIRE LIGHT INFANTRY
55009	**B**	DP	MBDL	BH		ALYCIDON
55016	**GG**	LS	MBDL	MG (S)		GORDON HIGHLANDER
55022	**B**	LS	LSLO	CL		ROYAL SCOTS GREY

CLASS 56   BRUSH/BR/RUSTON   Co-Co

Built: 1976–84 by Electroputere at Craiova, Romania (as sub-contractors for Brush) or BREL at Doncaster or Crewe Works.
Engine: Ruston Paxman 16RK3CT of 2460 kW (3250 hp) at 900 rpm.
Main Alternator: Brush BA1101A.
Traction Motors: Brush TM73-62.
Maximum Tractive Effort: 275 kN (61800 lbf).
Continuous Tractive Effort: 240 kN (53950 lbf) at 16.8 mph.
Power at Rail: 1790 kW (2400 hp).   **Train Brakes:** Air.
Brake Force: 60 t.   **Dimensions:** 19.36 x 2.79 m.
Weight: 126 t.   **Wheel Diameter:** 1143 mm.
Design Speed: 80 mph.   **Maximum Speed:** 80 mph.
Fuel Capacity: 5228 litres.   **Route Availability:** 7.
Train Supply: Not equipped.   **Total:** 21.

All equipped with Slow Speed Control.

Class 56s exported for use abroad are listed in section 5 of this book.

Most of the locomotives at Longport are being rebuilt as Class 69s.

Non-standard liveries:

56009 All over blue.
56303 All over dark green.

56009	**O**	EO	UKRS	LT (S)	
56049	**CS**	CS	COFS	NM	Robin of Templecombe 1938–2013
56051	**CS**	CS	COFS	NM	Survival
56077	**LH**	GB	UKRS	LT (S)	
56078	**CS**	CS	COFS	NM	
56081	**B**	GB	GBGD	LR	
56087	**CS**	BN	COFS	NM	
56090	**CS**	BN	COFS	NM	
56091	**DC**	DC	DCRO	LR	Driver Wayne Gaskell
					The Godfather
56094	**CS**	CS	COFS	NM	
56096	**CS**	BN	COFS	NM	
56097	**F**	EO		LT (S)	
56098	**BL**	GB	GBGD	LR	
56103	**DC**	DC	DCRS	LR (S)	
56104	**FO**	GB	UKRL	LT (S)	
56105	**CS**	BN	COFS	NM	
56113	**CS**	BN	COFS	NM	
56301 (56045)		**FA**	56	UKRL	LR
56302 (56124)		**CS**	CS	COFS	NM	PECO The Railway Modeller
					2016 70 Years
56303 (56125)		**O**	GB	HTLX	Willesden F Sdgs (S)
56312 (56003)		**DC**	GB	GBGD	LT (S)

CLASS 57   BRUSH/GM   Co-Co

Built: 1964–65 by Brush Traction at Loughborough or BR at Crewe Works as
Class 47. Rebuilt 1997–2004 by Brush Traction at Loughborough.
Engine: General Motors 12 645 E3 of 1860 kW (2500 hp) at 904 rpm.
Main Alternator: Brush BA1101D (recovered from Class 56).
Traction Motors: Brush TM64-68 Mark 1 or Mark 1A.
Maximum Tractive Effort: 244.5 kN (55000 lbf).
Continuous Tractive Effort: 140 kN (31500 lbf) at ?? mph.
Power at Rail: 1507 kW (2025 hp).   **Train Brakes:** Air.
Brake Force: 80 t.   **Dimensions:** 19.38 x 2.79 m.
Weight: 120.6 t.   **Wheel Diameter:** 1143 mm.
Design Speed: 75 mph.   **Maximum Speed:** 75 mph.
Fuel Capacity: 5550 litres.   **Route Availability:** 6
Train Supply: Not equipped.   **Total:** 32.

Non-standard liveries:

57311   LNWR lined black
57604   Original Great Western Railway green.

Class 57/0. No Train Supply Equipment. Rebuilt 1997–2000.

57001	(47356)	**WC**	WC	AWCA	CS (S)
57002	(47322)	**DI**	DR	XHSS	WS (S)	RAIL EXPRESS
57003	(47317)	**DR**	LS	LSLO	CL
57005	(47350)	**AZ**	WC	AWCX	CS (S)
57006	(47187)	**WC**	WC	AWCA	CS
57007	(47332)	**DI**	LS	LSLO	CL (S)
57008	(47060)	**DS**	WC	AWCA	CS (S)
57009	(47079)	**GG**	WC	AWCA	CS
57010	(47231)	**WC**	WC	AWCA	CS
57011	(47329)	**DS**	WC	AWCA	CS (S)
57012	(47204)	**WC**	WC	AWCA	CS

Class 57/3. Electric Train Supply Equipment. Former Virgin Trains locomotives fitted with retractable Dellner couplers. Rebuilt 2002–04. Details as Class 57/0 except:

Engine: General Motors 12645F3B of 2050 kW (2750 hp) at 954 rpm.
Main Alternator: Brush BA1101F (recovered from Class 56) or Brush BA1101G.
Fuel Capacity: 5887 litres.   **Train Supply:** Electric, index 100.
Design Speed: 95 mph.   **Maximum Speed:** 95 mph.
Brake Force: 60 t.   **Weight:** 117 t.

57301	(47845)	d	**DR**	P	XSDP	ZA (S)
57302	(47827)	d	**DS**	LS	LSLO	ZG (S)	Chad Varah
57303	(47705)	d	**DR**	P	XSDP	BH (S)	Pride of Carlisle
57304	(47807)	d	**DI**	DR	XHVT	KM	Pride of Cheshire
57305	(47822)	d	**DR**	P	GBBS	PG
57306	(47814)	d	**DI**	P	GBBS	PG	Her Majesty's Railway Inspectorate 175
57307	(47225)	d	**DI**	DR	XHVT	KM	LADY PENELOPE
57308	(47846)	d	**DI**	DR	XHVT	KM	Jamie Ferguson
57309	(47806)	d	**DI**	DR	XHVT	KM	Pride of Crewe
57310	(47831)	d	**DR**	P	GBBS	PG	Pride of Cumbria
57311	(47817)	d	**O**	LS	LSLO	CL
57312	(47330)	d	**RO**	P	EFOO	PZ
57313	(47371)		**PC**	WC	AWCA	CS	Scarborough Castle
57314	(47372)		**WC**	WC	AWCA	CS	Conwy Castle
57315	(47234)		**WC**	WC	AWCA	CS
57316	(47290)		**WC**	WC	AWCA	CS	Alnwick Castle

Class 57/6. Electric Train Supply Equipment. Prototype ETS loco. Rebuilt 2001. Details as Class 57/0 except:

Main Alternator: Brush BA1101E.   **Fuel Capacity:** 3273 litres.
Train Supply: Electric, index 95.   **Weight:** 113t.
Design Speed: 95 mph.   **Maximum Speed:** 95 mph.
Brake Force: 60 t.

57601	(47825)		**PC**	WC	AWCA	CS	Windsor Castle

Class 57/6. Electric Train Supply Equipment. Great Western Railway locomotives. Rebuilt 2004. Details as Class 57/3.

57602	(47337)	GW P	EFOO	PZ	Restormel Castle
57603	(47349)	GW P	EFOO	PZ	Tintagel Castle
57604	(47209)	O P	EFOO	PZ	PENDENNIS CASTLE
57605	(47206)	GW P	EFOO	PZ	Totnes Castle

CLASS 58   BREL/RUSTON   Co-Co

Built: 1983–87 by BREL at Doncaster Works.
Engine: Ruston Paxman 12RK3ACT of 2460 kW (3300 hp) at 1000 rpm.
Main Alternator: Brush BA1101B.
Traction Motors: Brush TM73-62.
Maximum Tractive Effort: 275 kN (61800 lbf).
Continuous Tractive Effort: 240 kN (53950 lbf) at 17.4 mph.
Power at Rail: 1780 kW (2387 hp).   **Train Brakes:** Air.
Brake Force: 60 t.   **Dimensions:** 19.13 x 2.72 m.
Weight: 130 t.   **Wheel Diameter:** 1120 mm.
Design Speed: 80 mph.   **Maximum Speed:** 80 mph.
Fuel Capacity: 4214 litres.   **Route Availability:** 7.
Train Supply: Not equipped.   **Total:** 2.

All equipped with Slow Speed Control.

Class 58s exported for use abroad are listed in section 5 of this book.

58012	F	PO	BL (S)	
58016	ML	PO	LR (S)	
58023	ML	PO	LR (S)	

CLASS 59   GENERAL MOTORS   Co-Co

Built: 1985 (59001–004) or 1989 (59005) by General Motors, La Grange, Illinois, USA or 1990 (59101–104), 1994 (59201) and 1995 (59202–206) by General Motors, London, Ontario, Canada.
Engine: General Motors 16-645E3C two stroke of 2460 kW (3300 hp) at 904 rpm.
Main Alternator: General Motors AR11 MLD-D14A.
Traction Motors: General Motors D77B.
Maximum Tractive Effort: 506 kN (113550 lbf).
Continuous Tractive Effort: 291 kN (65300 lbf) at 14.3 mph.
Power at Rail: 1889 kW (2533 hp).   **Train Brakes:** Air.
Brake Force: 69 t.   **Dimensions:** 21.35 x 2.65 m.
Weight: 121 t.   **Wheel Diameter:** 1067 mm.
Design Speed: 60 (* 75) mph.   **Maximum Speed:** 60 (* 75) mph.
Fuel Capacity: 4546 litres.   **Route Availability:** 7.
Train Supply: Not equipped.   **Total:** 15.

Class 59/0. Owned by Freightliner and GB Railfreight.

59001	**AI**	FL	DFHG	MD	YEOMAN ENDEAVOUR
59002	**AI**	FL	DFHG	MD	ALAN J DAY
59003	**GB**	GB	GBYH	RR	YEOMAN HIGHLANDER
59004	**AI**	FL	DFHG	MD	PAUL A HAMMOND
59005	**AI**	FL	DFHG	MD	KENNETH J PAINTER

Class 59/1. Owned by Freightliner.

59101	**HA**	FL	DFHG	MD	Village of Whatley
59102	**HA**	FL	DFHG	MD	Village of Chantry
59103	**HA**	FL	DFHG	MD	Village of Mells
59104	**HA**	FL	DFHG	MD	Village of Great Elm

Class 59/2. Owned by Freightliner.

59201	*	**DB**	FL	DFHG	MD	
59202	*	**FG**	FL	DFHG	MD	Pride of Ferrybridge
59203	*	**FG**	FL	DFHG	MD	
59204	*	**FG**	FL	DFHG	MD	
59205	*b	**FG**	FL	DFHG	MD	
59206	*b	**FG**	FL	DFHG	MD	John F. Yeoman Rail Pioneer

CLASS 60   BRUSH/MIRRLEES   Co-Co

Built: 1989–93 by Brush Traction at Loughborough.
Engine: Mirrlees 8MB275T of 2310 kW (3100 hp) at 1000 rpm.
Main Alternator: Brush BA1006A.
Traction Motors: Brush TM2161A.
Maximum Tractive Effort: 500 kN (106500 lbf).
Continuous Tractive Effort: 336 kN (71570 lbf) at 17.4 mph.
Power at Rail: 1800 kW (2415 hp).   **Train Brakes:** Air.
Brake Force: 74 t (+ 62 t).   **Dimensions:** 21.34 x 2.64 m.
Weight: 129 t (+ 131 t).   **Wheel Diameter:** 1118 mm.
Design Speed: 62 mph.   **Maximum Speed:** 60 mph.
Fuel Capacity: 4546 (+ 5225) litres.   **Route Availability:** 8.
Train Supply: Not equipped.   **Total:** 97.

All equipped with Slow Speed Control.

* Refurbished locomotives.

60034 carries its name on one side only.

60500 originally carried the number 60016.

Non-standard and Advertising liveries:

60028   Cappagh (blue).
60062   Steel on steel (various colours).
60066   Powering Drax (silver).
60074   Puma Energy (grey).
60081   Original Great Western Railway green.
60099   Tata Steel (silver).

60001	*	**DB**	DB	WCAT	TO	
60002	+*	**GB**	BN	GBTG	TO	GRAHAM FARISH 50TH ANNIVERSARY 1970–2020
60003	+	**E**	DB	WQCA	TO (S)	FREIGHT TRANSPORT ASSOCIATION
60004	+	**E**	GB	WQCA	TO (S)	
60005	+	**E**	DB	WQCA	TO (S)	
60007	+*	**DB**	DB	WCBT	TO	The Spirit of Tom Kendell
60008		**E**	DC	DCRS	LB (S)	
60009	+	**E**	DC	DCRS	LB (S)	
60010	+*	**DB**	DB	WCBT	TO	
60011		**DB**	DB	WQBA	TO (S)	
60012	+	**E**	DB	WQDA	TO (S)	
60013		**EG**	DC	DCRS	LB (S)	
60014		**EG**	GB	WQCA	TO (S)	
60015	+*	**DB**	DB	WCBT	TO	
60017	+*	**DB**	DB	WCBT	TO	
60018		**E**	GB	WQCA	TO (S)	
60019	*	**DB**	DB	WQBA	TO (S)	Port of Grimsby & Immingham
60020	+*	**DB**	DB	WQBA	TO (S)	The Willows
60021	+*	**GB**	BN	GBTG	TO	PENYGHENT
60022	+	**E**	DC	DCRS	LB (S)	
60023	+	**E**	DB	WQCA	TO (S)	
60024	*	**DB**	DB	WCAT	TO	Clitheroe Castle
60025	+	**E**	DB	WQCA	TO (S)	
60026	+*	**BN**	BN	GBTG	TO	HELVELLYN
60027	+	**E**	DB	WQCA	TO (S)	
60028	+	**0**	DC	DCRO	TO	
60029		**DC**	DC	DCRO	TO	Ben Nevis
60030	+	**E**	DB	WQCA	TO (S)	
60031		**E**	DB	WQCA	TO (S)	
60032		**F**	DB	WQDA	TO (S)	
60033	+	**CU**	DB	WQCA	TO (S)	Tees Steel Express
60034		**EG**	DB	WQCA	TO (S)	Carnedd Llewelyn
60035		**E**	DB	WQCA	TO (S)	
60036		**E**	DB	WQDA	TO (S)	GEFCO
60037	+	**E**	DB	WQDA	TO (S)	
60038	+	**E**	DC	DCRS	LB (S)	
60039	*	**DB**	DB	WQBA	TO (S)	Dove Holes
60040	*	**DB**	DB	WCAT	TO	The Territorial Army Centenary
60041	+	**E**	DB	WQCA	TO (S)	
60042		**E**	DB	WQCA	TO (S)	
60043		**E**	DB	WQCA	TO (S)	
60044	*	**DB**	DB	WCAT	TO	Dowlow
60045		**E**	DB	WQCA	TO (S)	The Permanent Way Institution
60046	+	**DC**	DC	DCRO	TO	William Wilberforce
60047	*	**CS**	BN	GBTG	TO	
60048		**E**	DB	WQDA	TO (S)	
60049		**E**	DB	WQCA	TO (S)	
60051	+	**E**	DB	WQCA	TO (S)	
60052	+	**E**	DB	WQDA	TO (S)	Glofa Twr – The last deep mine in Wales – Tower Colliery

60053		E	DB	WQCA	TO (S)	
60054	+*	DB	DB	WQBA	TO (S)	
60055	+	DC	DC	DCRO	TO	Thomas Barnardo
60056	+*	CS	BN	GBTG	TO	
60057		EG	DC	DCRS	LB (S)	
60058	+	E	DB	WQCA	TO (S)	
60059	+*	DB	DB	WCBT	TO	Swinden Dalesman
60060		EG	DC	DCRS	LR (S)	
60061		F	DC	DCRS	LB (S)	
60062	*	O	DB	WCAT	TO	Sonia
60063	*	DB	DB	WQBA	TO (S)	
60064	+	EG	DC	DCRS	LB (S)	
60065		E	DB	WQBA	TO (S)	Spirit of JAGUAR
60066	*	AL	DB	WCAT	TO	
60067		EG	DB	WQCA	TO (S)	
60068		EG	DB	WQDA	TO (S)	
60069		E	DB	WQCA	TO (S)	Slioch
60070	+	F	DC	DCRS	LB (S)	
60071	+	E	DB	WQCA	TO (S)	Ribblehead Viaduct
60072		EG	DB	WQCA	TO (S)	
60073		EG	DB	WQDA	TO (S)	
60074	*	AL	DB	WCAT	TO	Luke
60075		E	DC	DCRS	LB (S)	
60076	*	CS	BN	GBTG	TO	Dunbar
60077	+	EG	DB	WQDA	TO (S)	
60078		ML	DB	WQDA	TO (S)	
60079	*	DB	DB	WQBA	TO (S)	
60080	+	E	DC	DCRS	LB (S)	
60081	+	O	LS	WQDA	TO (S)	
60082		EG	DB	WQCA	CE (S)	
60083		E	DB	WQCA	TO (S)	
60084		EG	DB	WQDA	TO (S)	
60085	*	GB	BN	GBTG	TO	
60087	*	GB	BN	GBTG	TO	
60088		F	DB	WQCA	TO (S)	
60089	+	E	DB	WQDA	TO (S)	
60090	+	EG	DC	DCRS	LB (S)	
60091	+*	DB	DB	WQBA	TO (S)	Barry Needham
60092	+*	DB	DB	WQBA	TO (S)	
60093		E	DB	WQDA	TO (S)	
60094		E	DB	WQCA	TO (S)	Rugby Flyer
60095	*	GB	BN	GBTG	TO	
60096	+*	CS	BN	GBTG	TO	
60097	+	E	DB	WQCA	TO (S)	
60098	+	E	DC	DCRS	LB (S)	
60099		AL	DC	DCRS	LR (S)	
60100	*	DB	DB	WCAT	TO	Midland Railway - Butterley
60500		E	DB	WQCA	TO (S)	

CLASS 66   GENERAL MOTORS/EMD   Co-Co

Built: 1998–2008 by General Motors/EMD, London, Ontario, Canada (Model JT42CWR (low emission locomotives Model JT42CWRM)) or 2013–16 by EMD/Progress Rail, Muncie, Indiana (66752–779).
Engine: General Motors 12N-710G3B-EC two stroke of 2385 kW (3200 hp) at 904 rpm. 66752–779 GM 12N-710G3B-T2.
Main Alternator: General Motors AR8/CA6.
Traction Motors: General Motors D43TR.
Maximum Tractive Effort: 409 kN (92000 lbf).
Continuous Tractive Effort: 260 kN (58390 lbf) at 15.9 mph.

Power at Rail: 1850 kW (2480 hp).	**Train Brakes:** Air.
Brake Force: 68 t.	**Dimensions:** 21.35 x 2.64 m.
Weight: 127 t.	**Wheel Diameter:** 1120 mm.
Design Speed: 87.5 mph.	**Maximum Speed:** 75 mph.
Fuel Capacity: 6550 litres.	**Route Availability:** 7.
Train Supply: Not equipped.	**Total:** 417.

All equipped with Slow Speed Control.

Class 66s previously used in the UK but now in use abroad are listed in section 5 of this book. Some of the DBC 66s moved to France return to Great Britain from time to time for maintenance or operational requirements.

66422 carries its name on one side only.

Class 66 delivery dates. The Class 66 design and delivery evolved over an 18-year period, with more than 400 locomotives delivered. For clarity the delivery dates (by year) for each batch of locomotives is as follows:

66001–250	EWS (now DB Cargo). 1998–2000 (some now in use in France or Poland, ten sold to GB Railfreight and five on long-term hire to DRS).
66301–305	Fastline. 2008. Later transferred to DRS and then in 2022 to GB Railfreight.
66306–316	GB Railfreight. Number series reserved for additional locomotives being imported from mainland Europe in 2023–24.
66401–410	DRS. 2003. Now in use with GB Railfreight or Colas Rail and renumbered 66733–737 and 66742–746 (66734[i] since scrapped).
66411–420	DRS. 2006. Now leased by Freightliner (66411/412/417 exported to Poland).
66421–430	DRS. 2007
66431–434	DRS. 2008
66501–505	Freightliner. 1999
66506–520	Freightliner. 2000
66521–525	Freightliner. 2000 (66521 since scrapped).
66526–531	Freightliner. 2001
66532–537	Freightliner. 2001
66538–543	Freightliner. 2001
66544–553	Freightliner. 2001
66554	Freightliner. 2002 (replacement for 66521).
66555–566	Freightliner. 2002

▲ RMS Locotec-liveried 08754 shunts Transport for Wales DMU 197102 into Wolverton Works on 19/06/23.   **Mark Beal**

▼ Brand new Beacon Rail-liveried 18012 and 18011 are seen stored at Wolverton Works on 26/05/23.   **Mark Beal**

▲ LUL maroon-liveried 20142 and BR green 20007 pass Saxilby with 6Z35 13.05 Doncaster–Derby RTC wagon movement on 04/02/22. **Robert Pritchard**

▼ BR blue-liveried 31128 shunts stock at Pickering on the North Yorkshire Moors Railway on 09/06/23. **Andy Chard**

▲ West Coast Railway Company-liveried 33029 and 33025 clear the summit at Whiteball with a Burton-on-Trent–Paignton railtour on 29/05/23. **Stephen Ginn**

▼ Colas Rail-liveried 37099 hauls 1Q50 13.43 Derby RTC–Doncaster test train through Barnetby on 29/06/23. **Jonathan Longbottom**

▲ Europhoenix-liveried 37608 and 37510 top-and-tail London Overground EMU 710374 through Sheffield on a 5Q99 Derby–Derby turning movement on 03/10/22.
Robert Pritchard

▲ BR green-liveried 40145 is seen at Crewe on 12/11/22. **Stuart Hood**

▼ ScotRail InterCity-liveried 43168 and 43003 pass Bishopbriggs shortly after departure from Glasgow Queen Street with the 08.41 to Aberdeen on 09/06/23.
Robert Pritchard

▲ Rail Adventure-liveried HST power cars 43484 and 43465 pass Clay Cross on 20/03/23 hauling Railvac 3 as 6X43 10.03 Tyne Yard–Butterley. **Robert Pritchard**

▼ BR blue-liveried 47749 approaches Eastleigh hauling South Western Railway EMU 701055 from Derby to Eastleigh depot on 10/08/23. **Steve Stubbs**

▲ GB Railfreight-liveried 50007 is seen on display at Long Marston on 22/06/23. **Ian Beardsley**

▼ BR blue-liveried 55009 approaches Sheffield with the 06.57 Willington–London King's Cross "Capital Deltic Reprise" railtour on 29/07/23. **Robert Pritchard**

▲ Colas Rail-liveried 56096 is seen at Nottingham with 0Z41 12.08 Doncaster–Nottingham Eastcroft depot light engine move on 12/06/23. **Robert Pritchard**

▼ Pullman Car Company-liveried 57313 is seen at Powderham, between Dawlish and Exeter, with the 17.30 Paignton–Birmingham International Northern Belle on 22/08/23. **Robin Ralston**

▲ Hanson Quarry Products-liveried 59104 and Freightliner-liveried 66589 pass Langley with 7A09 07.18 Merehead–Acton on 18/10/22. **Robert Pritchard**

▼ Cappagh-liveried 60028 is seen at Dove Holes quarry on 27/07/23. **Steve Stubbs**

▲ In retro 1980s style two-tone trainload freight grey with Petroleum logos, GB Railfreight 66794 passes Ashford (Surrey) with 6Y26 10.51 Newhaven Marine–Woking loaded sand.

Robert Pritchard

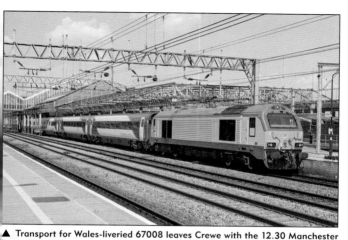

▲ Transport for Wales-liveried 67008 leaves Crewe with the 12.30 Manchester Piccadilly–Cardiff Central on 16/06/23. **Andy Chard**

▼ DRS (Class 68 style)-liveried 68001 and 68018 top-and-tail 6Z95 15.51 Winfrith–Crewe at Dorchester South on 20/04/23. **Stephen Ginn**

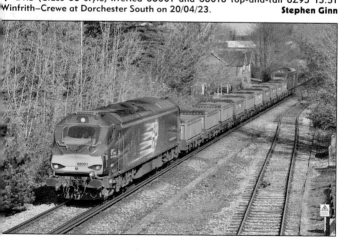

▲ GB Railfreight-liveried 69001 is seen near Feltham with 6Y42 14.05 Hoo Junction–Eastleigh on 16/08/23. **Tom McAtee**

▼ Freightliner-liveried 70001 passes Slindon, Staffordshire with 4M58 Southampton–Garston intermodal on 03/04/23. **Brad Joyce**

▲ BR Civil Engineers-liveried 73119 and Southern-liveried 73202 pass Maidstone East with the 10.55 Tonbridge–Nottingham Branch Line Society railtour on 11/06/23. **Robert Pritchard**

▼ BR InterCity-liveried 86101 hauls a 5Z91 London Euston–Crewe stock movement past Slindon, Staffordshire on 14/05/23. **Brad Joyce**

New DRS-liveried 88002 passes Wandel with 4Z27 08.40 Mossend–Daventry intermodal on 08/10/22. **Robin Ralston**

▲ New Freightliner-liveried 90008 and 90013 pass Castlethorpe, near Milton Keynes, with 4M87 11.13 Felixstowe–Trafford Park intermodal on 19/04/23.

Mark Beal

▼ LNER oxblood-liveried 91114 leaves Newark North Gate with the 14.03 London King's Cross–Leeds on 07/05/23.

Ian Beardsley

▲ Caledonian Sleeper-liveried 92038 is seen at London Euston after arrival with the Lowland Sleeper from Scotland on 17/06/23. **Robert Pritchard**

▼ Eurotunnel Class 9/7 freight shuttle locomotive 9701 leaves the Cheriton Eurotunnel terminus (Folkestone) with another lorry shuttle for Coquelles (Calais) on 08/04/23. **Robert Pritchard**

66567–574	Freightliner. 2003. 66573–574 now used by Colas Rail and renumbered 66846–847.
66575–577	Freightliner. 2004. Now used by Colas Rail and renumbered 66848–850.
66578–581	Freightliner. 2005. Now used by GBRf and renumbered 66738–741.
66582–594	Freightliner. 2007 (66582/583/584/586 exported to Poland).
66595–599	Freightliner. 2008 (66595 exported to Poland).
66601–606	Freightliner. 2000
66607–612	Freightliner. 2002 (66607/609/611/612 exported to Poland)
66613–618	Freightliner. 2003
66619–622	Freightliner. 2005
66623–625	Freightliner. 2007 (66624/625 exported to Poland).
66701–707	GB Railfreight. 2001
66708–712	GB Railfreight. 2002
66713–717	GB Railfreight. 2003
66718–722	GB Railfreight. 2006
66723–727	GB Railfreight. 2006
66728–732	GB Railfreight. 2008
66734[11]	GB Railfreight. Imported from mainland Europe in 2021.
66747–749	Built in 2008 as 20078968-004/006/007 (DE 6313/15/16) for Crossrail AG in the Netherlands but never used. Sold to GB Railfreight in 2012.
66750–751	Built in 2003 as 20038513-01/04 and have worked in the Netherlands, Germany and Poland. GBRf secured these two locomotives on lease in 2013.
66752–772	GB Railfreight. 2014
66773–779	GB Railfreight. 2016
66780–789	GB Railfreight. 1998–2000. Former DBC locomotives acquired in 2017 that have been renumbered in the GBRf number series.
66790–792	Built in 2002 as 20018352-3/4/5 (T66403–405) for CargoNet, Norway. Sold to Beacon Rail and leased to GBRf from 2019.
66793–799	Second-hand locos imported from mainland Europe in 2020–21 for GB Railfreight.
66951–952	Freightliner. 2004
66953–957	Freightliner. 2008 (66954 exported to Poland).

Advertising and non-standard liveries:

66004	I am a Climate Hero (green).
66109	PD Ports (dark blue).
66587	Ocean Network Express (pink with white stripes).
66708	**GB** livery with the addition of a large Ukraine flag.
66709	MSC – blue with images of a container ship.
66718	London Underground 150 (black).
66720	Wascosa blue with orange cabsides.
66721	London Underground 150 (white with tube map images). Also carries the numbers 1933 and 2013.
66723	Also carries the number ZA723.
66731	Thank you NHS (blue with orange cabsides).
66734	Platinum Jubilee (purple).
66747	Newell & Wright (blue, white & red).
66769	Prostate Cancer UK (black with blue lettering).

66775	Also carries the number F231.
66779	BR dark green.
66780	Cemex (grey, blue & red).
66783	Biffa (red & orange).
66793	Two-tone trainload freight grey with Construction decals.
66794	Two-tone trainload freight grey with Petroleum decals.
66796	It's Cleaner by Rail (green & blue).
66797	Beacon Rail (all-over blue with yellow solebar stripe and large yellow circle logo).

Class 66/0. DB Cargo-operated locomotives.

All fitted with Swinghead Automatic "Buckeye" Combination Couplers except 66001 and 66002.

66031, 66091, 66108, 66122 and 66126 are on long-term hire to DRS.

† Fitted with additional lights and drawgear for Lickey banking duties.

t Fitted with tripcocks for working over London Underground tracks between Harrow-on-the-Hill and Amersham.

66001 t	**DB**	DB	WBAE	TO	
66002	**E**	DB	WBAE	TO	
66003	**E**	DB	WBAE	TO	
66004	**AL**	DB	WBAR	TO	
66005	**MT**	DB	WBAE	TO	Maritime Intermodal One
66006	**E**	DB	WBAR	TO	
66007	**DB**	DB	WBAR	TO	
66009	**DB**	DB	WBAE	TO	
66010	**DB**	DB	WBRT	TO	
66011	**E**	DB	WBAE	TO	
66012	**DB**	DB	WBAE	TO	
66013	**E**	DB	WBAE	TO	
66014	**DB**	DB	WBAR	TO	
66015	**E**	DB	WBAE	TO	
66017 t	**DB**	DB	WBAR	TO	
66018	**DB**	DB	WQBA	TO (S)	
66019 t	**DB**	DB	WBAE	TO	
66020	**DB**	DB	WBAE	TO	
66021	**DB**	DB	WBAR	TO	
66023	**E**	DB	WBAT	TO	
66024	**E**	DB	WBAE	TO	
66025	**DB**	DB	WBRT	TO	
66026	**E**	DB	WBAI	TO (S)	
66027	**DB**	DB	WBAE	TO	
66028	**E**	DB	WBAE	TO	
66030	**E**	DB	WBAR	TO	
66031	**DR**	DB	XHIM	KM	
66032	**DB**	DB	WBAE	TO	
66034	**DB**	DB	WBAE	TO	
66035	**DB**	DB	WBAE	TO	Resourceful
66037	**E**	DB	WQBA	TO (S)	
66039	**DB**	DB	WBET	TO	

66040	E	DB	WBAR	TO	
66041	DB	DB	WBRT	TO	
66043	E	DB	WQBA	TO (S)	
66044	DB	DB	WBRT	TO	
66047	MT	DB	WBAE	TO	Maritime Intermodal Two
66050	DB	DB	WBAE	TO	
66051	MT	DB	WBAR	TO	Maritime Intermodal Four
66053	E	DB	WBAE	TO	
66054	DB	DB	WBAR	TO	
66055 †	DB	DB	WBLE	TO	Alain Thauvette
66056 †	DB	DB	WBLE	TO	
66057 †	E	DB	WBLE	TO	
66059 †	E	DB	WBLE	TO	
66060	E	DB	WBAR	TO	
66061	DB	DB	WBAE	TO	
66063	E	DB	WBRT	TO	
66065	DB	DB	WBAR	TO	
66066	DB	DB	WBAR	TO	Geoff Spencer
66067	E	DB	WBAE	TO	
66068	E	DB	WBRT	TO	
66069	DB	DB	WBAE	TO	
66070	DB	DB	WBRT	TO	
66073	DB	DB	WBAE	TO	
66074	DB	DB	WBAE	TO	
66075	E	DB	WBAE	TO	
66076	E	DB	WBAE	TO	
66077	DB	DB	WBAR	TO	Benjamin Gimbert G.C.
66078	DB	DB	WBAE	TO	
66079	DB	DB	WBAR	TO	James Nightall G.C.
66080	E	DB	WBAE	TO	
66082	DB	DB	WBAE	TO	
66083	E	DB	WBAR	TO	
66084	DB	DB	WBAE	TO	
66085	DB	DB	WBRT	TO	
66086	DB	DB	WBAE	TO	
66087	E	DB	WBAE	TO	
66088	DB	DB	WBAE	TO	
66089	E	DB	WBAR	TO	
66090	MT	DB	WBAE	TO	Maritime Intermodal Six
66091	DR	DB	XHIM	KM	
66092	E	DB	WBRT	TO	
66093	DB	DB	WBAE	TO	
66094	DB	DB	WBAE	TO	
66095	E	DB	WBAE	TO	
66096	E	DB	WBAE	TO	
66097	DB	DB	WBRT	TO	
66098	E	DB	WBAE	TO	
66099 r	DB	DB	WBBE	TO	
66100 r	DB	DB	WBBE	TO	Armistice 100 1918–2018
66101 r	DB	DB	WBBE	TO	
66102 r	DB	DB	WBBE	TO	

66103 r	E	DB	WBBE	TO	
66104 r	DB	DB	WBRT	TO	
66105 r	DB	DB	WBBE	TO	
66106 r	E	DB	WBBE	TO	
66107 r	DB	DB	WBRT	TO	
66108 r	DR	DB	XHIM	KM	
66109	AL	DB	WBAR	TO	Teesport Express
66110 r	E	DB	WBBE	TO	
66111 r	E	DB	WBBE	TO	
66112 r	E	DB	WBBE	TO	
66113 r	DB	DB	WBRT	TO	
66114 r	DB	DB	WBBE	TO	
66115	DB	DB	WBAE	TO	
66116	E	DB	WBAE	TO	
66117	DB	DB	WBAE	TO	
66118	DB	DB	WBAE	TO	
66119	E	DB	WBAE	TO	
66120	E	DB	WBAE	TO	
66121	E	DB	WBAE	TO	
66122	DR	DB	XHIM	KM	
66124	DB	DB	WBAR	TO	
66125	DB	DB	WBAE	TO	
66126	DR	DB	XHIM	KM	
66127	E	DB	WBAE	TO	
66128	DB	DB	WBAE	TO	
66129	E	DB	WBAE	TO	
66130	DB	DB	WBRT	TO	
66131	DB	DB	WBAE	TO	
66133	E	DB	WBAE	TO	
66134	DB	DB	WBAE	TO	
66135	DB	DB	WBAE	TO	
66136	DB	DB	WBAE	TO	
66137	DB	DB	WBAE	TO	
66138	E	DB	WQBA	TO (S)	
66139	DB	DB	WBAE	TO	
66140	E	DB	WBAE	TO	
66142	MT	DB	WBAR	TO	Maritime Intermodal Three
66143	DB	DB	WBAE	TO	
66144	DB	DB	WBAR	TO	
66145	E	DB	WQBA	TO (S)	
66147	DB	DB	WBAE	TO	
66148	MT	DB	WBAE	TO	Maritime Intermodal Seven
66149	DB	DB	WBAE	TO	
66150	DB	DB	WBAE	TO	
66151	E	DB	WBAE	TO	
66152	DB	DB	WBAE	TO	Derek Holmes Railway Operator
66154	DB	DB	WBAE	TO	
66155	E	DB	WBRT	TO	
66156	DB	DB	WBAE	TO	
66158	E	DB	WBAE	TO	
66160	E	DB	WBAR	TO	

66161	E	DB	WBAE	TO	
66162	MT	DB	WBAR	TO	Maritime Intermodal Five
66164	E	DB	WBAE	TO	
66165	DB	DB	WBAR	TO	
66167	DB	DB	WBAE	TO	
66168	DB	DB	WBAR	TO	
66169	E	DB	WBAE	TO	
66170	E	DB	WBAE	TO	
66171	E	DB	WBAE	TO	
66172	E	DB	WBAE	TO	PAUL MELLENEY
66174	E	DB	WBAE	TO	
66175	DB	DB	WBAE	TO	Rail Riders Express
66176	E	DB	WBAR	TO	
66177	E	DB	WBAE	TO	
66179	E	DB	WBAE	TO	
66181	E	DB	WBAR	TO	
66182	DB	DB	WBAE	TO	
66183	E	DB	WBAE	TO	
66185	DB	DB	WBRT	TO	DP WORLD London Gateway
66186	E	DB	WBAE	TO	
66187	E	DB	WBAE	TO	
66188	E	DB	WBAR	TO	
66190	DB	DB	WBAE	TO	Martin House Children's Hospice
66192	DB	DB	WBAR	TO	
66194	E	DB	WBAR	TO	
66197	DB	DB	WBAE	TO	
66198	E	DB	WBAR	TO	
66199	E	DB	WBAE	TO	
66200	E	DB	WBAE	TO	
66205	DB	DB	WBAI	TO	
66206	DB	DB	WBAR	TO	
66207	E	DB	WBAE	TO	
66221	E	DB	WBAR	TO	
66224	E	DB	WBAI	TO (S)	
66230	DB	DB	WQCA	TO (S)	
66244	DB	DB	WBAE	TO	

Class 66/3. Former Fastline and DRS-operated locomotives now operated by GB Railfreight. Low emission. Details as Class 66/0 except:

Engine: EMD 12N-710G3B-T2 two stroke of 2420 kW (3245 hp) at 904 rpm.
Traction Motors: General Motors D43TRC.
Fuel Capacity: 5150 litres.

66301	r	DR	BN	GBLT	RR
66302	r	DR	BN	GBLT	RR
66303	r	DR	BN	GBLT	RR
66304	r	DR	BN	GBLT	RR
66305	r	DR	BN	GBLT	RR

Class 66/3. Number series reserved for further locomotives being sourced from mainland Europe for GB Railfreight. Locomotives are being delivered during 2023–24.

66306	(CB1001)	**GB**	AK	GBSD	RR	SCS Logistics
66307	(77502)	**GB**	AK	GBSD	RR	
66308	(77503)	**GB**	AK	GBSD	RR	
66309	(77501)	**GB**	AK	GBSD	RR	
66310	(77507)		AK		LB	
66311	(77504)		AK		LB	
66312	(266107)		AK		LB	
66313	(CB1000)		AK		LB	
66314	(77505)		AK			
66315	(77506)		AK			
66316	(29003)		AK			

Class 66/4. Low emission. Akiem-owned. Details as Class 66/3.

66413	**FG**	AK	DFIN	LD	Lest We Forget
66414	**FH**	AK	DFIN	LD	
66415	**FG**	AK	DFIN	LD	You Are Never Alone
66416	**FH**	AK	DFIN	LD	
66418	**FH**	AK	DFIN	LD	PATRIOT – IN MEMORY OF FALLEN RAILWAY EMPLOYEES
66419	**FG**	AK	DFIN	LD	Lionesses' Roar
66420	**FH**	AK	DFIN	LD	
66421	**DR**	AK	XHIM	KM	Gresty Bridge TMD
66422	**DR**	AK	XHIM	KM	Max Joule 1958–1999
66423	**DR**	AK	XHIM	KM	
66424	**DR**	AK	XHIM	KM	Driver Paul Scrivens 1969–2021
66425	**DR**	AK	XHIM	KM	Nigel J Kirchstein 1957–2021
66426	**DR**	AK	XHIM	KM	
66427	**DR**	AK	XHIM	KM	
66428	**DR**	AK	XHIM	KM	Carlisle Eden Mind
66429	**DR**	AK	XHIM	KM	
66430	**DR**	AK	XHIM	KM	
66431	**DR**	AK	XHIM	KM	
66432	**DR**	AK	XHIM	KM	
66433	**DR**	AK	XHIM	KM	
66434	**DR**	AK	XHIM	KM	Carlisle Power Signal Box 50th Anniversary 1973–2023

Class 66/5. Standard design. Freightliner-operated locomotives. Details as Class 66/0.

66501	**FL**	P	DFIM	LD	Japan 2001
66502	**FG**	P	DFIM	LD	Basford Hall Centenary 2001
66503	**FG**	P	DFIM	LD	The RAILWAY MAGAZINE Celebrating 125 years 1897–2022
66504	**FH**	P	DFIM	LD	
66505	**FL**	P	DFIM	LD	
66506	**FL**	E	DFIM	LD	Crewe Regeneration
66507	**FL**	E	DFIM	LD	
66508	**FG**	E	DFIM	LD	

66509	**FG**	E	DFIM	LD	Josiah's Wish
66510	**FL**	E	DFIM	LD	
66511	**FL**	E	DFIM	LD	
66512	**FL**	E	DFIM	LD	
66513	**FL**	E	DFIM	LD	
66514	**FL**	E	DFIM	LD	
66515	**FL**	E	DFIM	LD	
66516	**FL**	E	DFIM	LD	
66517	**FL**	E	DFIM	LD	
66518	**FL**	E	DFIM	LD	
66519	**FL**	E	DFIM	LD	
66520	**FL**	E	DFIM	LD	
66522	**FL**	E	DFIM	LD	
66523	**FL**	E	DFIM	LD	
66524	**FL**	E	DFIM	LD	
66525	**FL**	E	DFIM	LD	
66526	**FL**	P	DHLT	LD (S)	Driver Steve Dunn (George)
66528	**FH**	P	DFIM	LD	Madge Elliot MBE
					Borders Railway Opening 2015
66529	**FL**	P	DHLT	LD (S)	
66531	**FL**	P	DFIM	LD	
66532	**FL**	P	DFIM	LD	P&O Nedlloyd Atlas
66533	**FL**	P	DFIM	LD	Hanjin Express/Senator Express
66534	**FL**	P	DFIM	LD	OOCL Express
66536	**FL**	P	DFIM	LD	
66537	**FL**	P	DFIM	LD	
66538	**FL**	E	DFIM	LD	
66539	**FL**	E	DFIM	LD	
66540	**FL**	E	DFIM	LD	Ruby
66541	**FL**	E	DFIM	LD	
66542	**FL**	E	DFIM	LD	
66543	**FL**	E	DFIM	LD	
66544	**FL**	P	DFIM	LD	
66545	**FL**	P	DFIM	LD	
66546	**FL**	P	DFIM	LD	
66547	**FL**	P	DFIM	LD	
66548	**FL**	P	DFIM	LD	
66549	**FL**	P	DFIM	LD	
66550	**FL**	P	DFIM	LD	
66551	**FL**	P	DFIM	LD	
66552	**FL**	P	DFIM	LD	Maltby Raider
66553	**FL**	P	DFIM	LD	
66554	**FL**	E	DFIM	LD	
66555	**FL**	E	DFIM	LD	
66556	**FL**	E	DFIM	LD	
66557	**FL**	E	DFIM	LD	
66558	**FL**	E	DFIM	LD	
66559	**FL**	E	DFIM	LD	
66560	**FL**	E	DFIM	LD	
66561	**FL**	E	DFIM	LD	
66562	**FL**	E	DFIM	LD	

66563	**FL**	E	DFIM	LD	
66564	**FL**	E	DFIM	LD	
66565	**FL**	E	DFIM	LD	
66566	**FL**	E	DFIM	LD	
66567	**FL**	E	DFIM	LD	
66568	**FL**	E	DFIM	LD	
66569	**FL**	E	DFIM	LD	
66570	**FL**	E	DFIM	LD	
66571	**FL**	E	DFIM	LD	
66572	**FL**	E	DFIM	LD	

Class 66/5. Freightliner-operated low emission locomotives. Details as Class 66/3.

66585	**FL**	HX	DFIN	LD	
66587	**AL**	HX	DFIN	LD	AS ONE, WE CAN
66588	**FL**	HX	DFIN	LD	
66589	**FL**	HX	DFIN	LD	
66590	**FL**	HX	DFIN	LD	
66591	**FL**	HX	DFIN	LD	
66592	**FL**	HX	DFIN	LD	Johnson Stevens Agencies
66593	**FL**	HX	DFIN	LD	3MG MERSEY MULTIMODAL GATEWAY
66594	**FL**	HX	DFIN	LD	NYK Spirit of Kyoto
66596	**FL**	BN	DFIN	LD	
66597	**FL**	BN	DFIN	LD	Viridor
66598	**FL**	BN	DFIN	LD	
66599	**FL**	BN	DHLT	LD (S)	

Class 66/6. Freightliner-operated locomotives with modified gear ratios.
Details as Class 66/0 except:
Maximum Tractive Effort: 467 kN (105080 lbf).
Continuous Tractive Effort: 296 kN (66630 lbf) at 14.0 mph.
Design Speed: 65 mph.   **Maximum Speed**: 65 mph.

66601	**FL**	P	DFHH	LD	The Hope Valley
66602	**FL**	P	DFHH	LD	
66603	**FL**	P	DFHH	LD	
66604	**FL**	P	DFHH	LD	
66605	**FG**	P	DFHH	LD	
66606	**FL**	P	DFHH	LD	
66607	**FL**	P	DFHH	LD	
66610	**FL**	P	DFHH	LD	
66613	**FL**	E	DFHH	LD	
66614	**FL**	E	DFHH	LD	1916 POPPY 2016
66615	**FL**	E	DFHH	LD	
66616	**FL**	E	DFHH	LD	
66617	**FL**	E	DFHH	LD	
66618	**FL**	E	DFHH	LD	Railways Illustrated Annual Photographic Awards Alan Barnes
66619	**FL**	E	DFHH	LD	Derek W. Johnson MBE
66620	**FL**	E	DFHH	LD	
66621	**FL**	E	DFHH	LD	
66622	**FL**	E	DFHH	LD	

Class 66/6. Freightliner-operated low emission locomotive with modified gear ratios. Details as Class 66/6 except:

Fuel Capacity: 5150 litres.

66623	**FG**	AK	DFHH		LD	

Class 66/7. Standard design. GB Railfreight-operated locomotives. Details as Class 66/0 except 66793–796 which are as Class 66/6.

66701	**GB**	E	GBBT	RR	
66702	**GB**	E	GBBT	RR	Blue Lightning
66703	**GB**	E	GBBT	RR	Doncaster PSB 1981–2002
66704	**GB**	E	GBBT	RR	Colchester Power Signalbox
66705	**GB**	E	GBBT	RR	Golden Jubilee
66706	**GB**	E	GBBT	RR	Nene Valley
66707	**GB**	E	GBBT	RR	Sir Sam Fay GREAT CENTRAL RAILWAY
66708	**O**	E	GBBT	RR	Слава УкраÏнi/Glory to Ukraine
66709	**AL**	E	GBBT	RR	Sorrento
66710	**GB**	E	GBBT	RR	Phil Packer BRIT
66711	**AI**	E	GBBT	RR	Sence
66712	**GB**	E	GBBT	RR	Peterborough Power Signalbox
66713	**GB**	E	GBBT	RR	Forest City
66714	**GB**	E	GBBT	RR	Cromer Lifeboat
66715	**GB**	E	GBBT	RR	VALOUR – IN MEMORY OF ALL RAILWAY EMPLOYEES WHO GAVE THEIR LIVES FOR THEIR COUNTRY
66716	**GB**	E	GBBT	RR	LOCOMOTIVE & CARRIAGE INSTITUTION CENTENARY 1911–2011
66717	**GB**	E	GBBT	RR	Good Old Boy

66718–751. GB Railfreight locomotives.

Details as Class 66/0 except 66718–732/747–749 as below:

Engine: EMD 12N-710G3B-T2 two stroke of 2420 kW (3245 hp) at 904 rpm.
Traction Motors: General Motors D43TRC.
Fuel Capacity: 5546 litres (66718–722) or 5150 litres (66723–732/747–749).

66747–749 were originally built for Crossrail AG in the Netherlands.

66750/751 were originally built for mainland Europe in 2003.

66718	**AL**	E	GBLT	RR	Peter, Lord Hendy of Richmond Hill of Imber in the County of Wiltshire
66719	**GB**	E	GBLT	RR	METRO-LAND
66720	**O**	E	GBLT	RR	wascosa
66721	**AL**	E	GBLT	RR	Harry Beck
66722	**GB**	E	GBLT	RR	Sir Edward Watkin
66723	**GB**	E	GBLT	RR	Chinook
66724	**GB**	E	GBLT	RR	Drax Power Station
66725	**GB**	E	GBLT	RR	SUNDERLAND
66726	**GB**	E	GBLT	RR	SHEFFIELD WEDNESDAY
66727	**MT**	E	GBLT	RR	Maritime One
66728	**GB**	P	GBLT	RR	Institution of Railway Operators
66729	**GB**	P	GBLT	RR	DERBY COUNTY

66730	**GB**	P	GBLT		RR	Whitemoor
66731	**AL**	P	GBLT		RR	Capt. Tom Moore
						A True British Inspiration
66732	**GB**	P	GBLT		RR	GBRf The First Decade 1999–2009
						John Smith – MD
66733 (66401) r	**GB**	P	GBFM		RR	Cambridge PSB
66734[11](PB04)	**O**	BN	GBEB		RR	PLATINUM JUBILEE
66735 (66403)	**GB**	P	GBBT		RR	PETERBOROUGH UNITED
66736 (66404) r	**GB**	P	GBFM		RR	WOLVERHAMPTON WANDERERS
66737 (66405) r	**GB**	P	GBFM		RR	Lesia
66738 (66578)	**GB**	BN	GBBT		RR	HUDDERSFIELD TOWN
66739 (66579) r	**GB**	BN	GBFM		RR	Bluebell Railway
66740 (66580) r	**GB**	BN	GBFM		RR	Sarah
66741 (66581)	**GB**	BN	GBBT		RR	Swanage Railway
66742 (66406, 66841)	**GB**	BN	GBBT		RR	ABP Port of Immingham
						Centenary 1912–2012
66743 (66407, 66842) r	**M**	BN	GBFM		RR	
66744 (66408, 66843)	**GB**	BN	GBBT		RR	Crossrail
66745 (66409, 66844)	**GB**	BN	GBRT		RR	
66746 (66410, 66845) r	**M**	BN	GBFM		RR	
66747 (20078968-007)	**AL**	BN	GBEB		RR	Made in Sheffield
66748 (20078968-004)	**GB**	BN	GBEB		RR	West Burton 50
66749 (20078968-006)	**GB**	BN	GBEB		RR	Christopher Hopcroft MBE
						60 Years Railway Service
66750 (20038513-01)	**GB**	BN	GBEB		RR	Bristol Panel Signal Box
66751 (20038513-04) c	**GB**	BN	GBEB		RR	Inspiration Delivered
						Hitachi Rail Europe

66752–779. Low emission, new build GB Railfreight locomotives. Details as Class 66/3.

66752	**GB**	GB	GBEL		RR	The Hoosier State
66753	**GB**	GB	GBEL		RR	EMD Roberts Road
66754	**GB**	GB	GBEL		RR	Northampton Saints
66755	**GB**	GB	GBEL		RR	Tony Berkeley OBE
						RFG Chairman 1997–2018
66756	**GB**	GB	GBEL		RR	Royal Corps of Signals
66757	**GB**	GB	GBEL		RR	West Somerset Railway
66758	**GB**	GB	GBEL		RR	The Pavior
66759	**GB**	GB	GBEL		RR	Chippy
66760	**GB**	GB	GBEL		RR	David Gordon Harris
66761	**GB**	GB	GBEL		RR	Wensleydale Railway Association
						25 Years 1990–2015
66762	**GB**	GB	GBEL		RR	
66763	**GB**	GB	GBEL		RR	Severn Valley Railway
66764	**GB**	GB	GBEL		RR	Major John Poyntz Engineer &
						Railwayman
66765	**GB**	GB	GBEL		RR	Julia Garn
66766	**GB**	GB	GBEL		RR	Gail Richardson
66767	**GB**	GB	GBEL		RR	King's Cross PSB 1971–2021

66768	**GB**	GB	GBEL	RR	
66769	**AL**	GB	GBEL	RR	LMA LEAGUE MANAGERS ASSOCIATION/ Paul Taylor Our Inspiration
66770	**GB**	GB	GBEL	RR	
66771	**GB**	GB	GBEL	RR	Amanda
66772	**GB**	GB	GBEL	RR	Maria
66773	**GB**	GB	GBNB	RR	Pride of GB Railfreight
66774	**GB**	GB	GBNB	RR	
66775	**GB**	GB	GBNB	RR	HMS Argyll
66776	**GB**	GB	GBNB	RR	Joanne
66777	**GB**	GB	GBNB	RR	Annette
66778	**GB**	GB	GBNB	RR	Cambois Depot 25 Years
66779	**0**	GB	GBEL	RR	EVENING STAR

66780–789. Standard design. Former DB Cargo locomotives acquired by GB Railfreight in 2017. Details as Class 66/0. Fitted with Swinghead Automatic "Buckeye" Combination Couplers.

† Fitted with additional lights and drawgear formerly used for Lickey banking duties.

66780 (66008)	**AL**	GB	GBOB	RR	The Cemex Express
66781 (66016)	**GB**	GB	GBOB	RR	Darius Cheskin
66782 (66046)	**GB**	GB	GBOB	RR	
66783 (66058) †	**AL**	GB	GBOB	RR	The Flying Dustman
66784 (66081)	**GB**	GB	GBOB	RR	Keighley & Worth Valley Railway 50th Anniversary 1968–2018
66785 (66132)	**GB**	GB	GBOB	RR	John Ellis
66786 (66141)	**GB**	GB	GBOB	RR	Cambridge University Railway Club Founded by Junior Members in 1911
66787 (66184)	**GB**	GB	GBOB	RR	Three Bridges ASC
66788 (66238)	**GB**	GB	GBOB	RR	LOCOMOTION 15
66789 (66250)	**BL**	GB	GBOB	RR	British Rail 1948–1997

66790–799. Locomotives sourced from mainland Europe.

66790 (T66403)	**GB**	BN	GBBT	RR	Louise
66791 (T66404)	**BN**	BN	GBBT	RR	
66792 (T66405)	**GB**	BN	GBBT	RR	Collaboration
66793 (29004)	**0**	BN	GBHH	RR	
66794 (29005)	**0**	BN	GBHH	RR	Steve Hannam
66795 (561-05)	**GB**	BN	GBHH	RR	Bescot LDC
66796 (561-01)	**AL**	BN	GBHH	RR	The Green Progressor
66797 (513-09)	**0**	BN	GBEB	RR	
66798 (561-03)	**GB**	BN	GBEB	RR	Justine
66799 (6602)	**GB**	BN	GBEB	RR	Modern Railways Diamond Jubilee

Class 66/8. Standard design. Colas Rail locomotives. Details as Class 66/0.

66846 (66573)	**CS**	BN	COLO	HJ	
66847 (66574)	**CS**	BN	COLO	HJ	Terry Baker
66848 (66575)	**CS**	BN	COLO	HJ	
66849 (66576)	**CS**	BN	COLO	HJ	Wylam Dilly
66850 (66577)	**CS**	BN	COLO	HJ	David Maidment OBE

Class 66/9. Freightliner locomotives. Low emission "demonstrator" locomotives. Details as Class 66/3. * **Fuel Capacity:** 5905 litres.

66951	*	**FL**	E	DFIN	LD
66952		**FL**	E	DFIN	LD

Class 66/5. Freightliner-operated low emission locomotives. Owing to the 665xx number range being full, subsequent deliveries of 66/5s were numbered from 66953 onwards. Details as Class 66/5 (low emission).

66953	**FL**	BN	DFIN	LD	
66955	**FL**	BN	DHLT	LD (S)	
66956	**FL**	BN	DHLT	LD (S)	
66957	**FL**	BN	DFIN	LD	Stephenson Locomotive Society 1909–2009

CLASS 67   ALSTOM/GENERAL MOTORS   Bo-Bo

Built: 1999–2000 by Alstom at Valencia, Spain, as sub-contractors for General Motors (General Motors model JT42 HW-HS).
Engine: GM 12N-710G3B-EC two stroke of 2385 kW (3200 hp) at 904 rpm.
Main Alternator: General Motors AR9A/HEP7/CA6C.
Traction Motors: General Motors D43FM.
Maximum Tractive Effort: 141 kN (31770 lbf).
Continuous Tractive Effort: 90 kN (20200 lbf) at 46.5 mph.

Power at Rail: 1860 kW.	**Train Brakes:** Air.
Brake Force: 78 t.	**Dimensions:** 19.74 x 2.72 m.
Weight: 90 t.	**Wheel Diameter:** 965 mm.
Design Speed: 125 mph.	**Maximum Speed:** 125 mph.
Fuel Capacity: 4927 litres.	**Route Availability:** 8.
Train Supply: Electric, index 66.	**Total:** 30.

All equipped with Slow Speed Control and Swinghead Automatic "Buckeye" Combination Couplers.

The following locomotives have been modified to operate with Transport for Wales Mark 4 stock: 67008, 67010, 67012, 67013, 67014, 67015, 67017, 67020, 67022, 67025, 67029.

Non-standard liveries:

67007 Platinum Jubilee (purple).
67026 Diamond Jubilee (silver).
67029 All over silver with DB logos.

67001		**AB**	DB	WQBA	CE (S)
67002		**DB**	DB	WEAC	CE
67003		**AB**	DB	WQBA	TO (S)
67004	r	**DB**	DB	WQBA	TO (S)
67005		**RZ**	DB	WAAC	CE	Queen's Messenger
67006		**RZ**	DB	WAAC	CE	Royal Sovereign
67007	r	**0**	DB	WABC	CE
67008		**TW**	DB	WAWC	CE
67009	r	**E**	DB	WQBA	CE (S)
67010		**DB**	DB	WAWC	CE

67011 r	**E**	DB	WQBA	CE (S)	
67012	**CM**	DB	WAWC	CE	
67013	**DB**	DB	WAWC	CE	
67014	**TW**	DB	WAWC	CE	
67015	**DB**	DB	WAWC	CE	
67016	**E**	DB	WAWC	CE	
67017	**TW**	DB	WAWC	CE	
67018	**DB**	DB	WQBA	CE (S)	Keith Heller
67019	**E**	DB	WQBA	TO (S)	
67020	**TB**	DB	WAWC	CE	
67021	**PC**	DB	WAAC	CE	
67022	**TB**	DB	WAWE	CE	
67023	**CS**	BN	GBKP	EC	Stella
67024	**PC**	DB	WAAC	CE	
67025	**TW**	DB	WAWC	CE	
67026	**O**	DB	WQBA	CE (S)	Diamond Jubilee
67027	**GB**	BN	COTS	RU	
67028	**DB**	DB	WAAC	CE	
67029	**O**	DB	WAWC	CE	Royal Diamond
67030 r	**E**	DB	WQBA	TO (S)	

CLASS 68   VOSSLOH/STADLER   Bo-Bo

New Vossloh/Stadler mixed-traffic locomotives operated by DRS.

Built: 2012–16 by Vossloh/Stadler, Valencia, Spain.
Engine: Caterpillar C175-16 of 2800 kW (3750 hp) at 1740 rpm.
Main Alternator: ABB WGX560.
Traction Motors: 4 x AMXL400 AC frame mounted ABB 4FRA6063.
Maximum Tractive Effort: 317 kN (71260 lbf).
Continuous Tractive Effort: 258 kN (58000 lbf) at 20.5 mph.

Power at Rail:	**Train Brakes:** Air & rheostatic.
Brake Force: 73 t.	**Dimensions:** 20.50 x 2.69 m.
Weight: 85 t.	**Wheel Diameter:** 1100 mm.
Design Speed: 100 mph.	**Maximum Speed:** 100 mph.
Fuel Capacity: 5600 litres.	**Route Availability:** 7.
Train Supply: Electric, index 96.	**Total:** 34.

68008–015 have been modified to operate in push-pull mode on the Chiltern Railways locomotive-hauled Mark 3 sets.

68019–034 have been modified to operate in push-pull mode with the TransPennine Express Mark 5A stock.

Non-standard and advertising liveries:

68006 Powering a greener Britain (dark & light green).
68014 On Track to a Greener Future (green & white).

68001	**DI**	BN	XHVE	CR	Evolution
68002	**DI**	BN	XHVE	CR	Intrepid
68003	**DI**	BN	XHVE	CR	Astute
68004	**DI**	BN	XHVE	CR	Rapid

68005	**DI**	BN	XHVE	CR	Defiant
68006	**0**	BN	XHVE	CR	Pride of the North
68007	**DR**	BN	XHVE	CR	Valiant
68008	**DI**	BN	XHCS	CR	Avenger
68009	**DI**	BN	XHCS	CR	Titan
68010	**CM**	BN	XHCE	CR	Oxford Flyer
68011	**CM**	BN	XHCE	CR	
68012	**CM**	BN	XHCE	CR	
68013	**CM**	BN	XHCE	CR	Peter Wreford-Bush
68014	**AL**	BN	XHCE	CR	
68015	**CM**	BN	XHCE	CR	Kev Helmer
68016	**DI**	BN	XHVE	CR	Fearless
68017	**DI**	BN	XHVE	CR	Hornet
68018	**DI**	BN	XHVE	CR	Vigilant
68019	**TP**	BN	TPEX	CR	Brutus
68020	**TP**	BN	TPEX	CR	Reliance
68021	**TP**	BN	TPEX	CR	Tireless
68022	**TP**	BN	TPEX	CR	Resolution
68023	**TP**	BN	TPEX	CR	Achilles
68024	**TP**	BN	TPEX	CR	Centaur
68025	**TP**	BN	TPEX	CR	Superb
68026	**TP**	BN	TPEX	CR	Enterprise
68027	**TP**	BN	TPEX	CR	Splendid
68028	**TP**	BN	TPEX	CR	Lord President
68029	**TP**	BN	TPEX	CR	Courageous
68030	**TP**	BN	TPEX	CR	Black Douglas
68031	**TP**	BN	TPEX	CR	Felix
68032	**TP**	BN	TPEX	CR	Destroyer
68033	**DI**	DR	XHTP	CR	The Poppy
68034	**DI**	DR	XHTP	CR	Rail Riders 2020

CLASS 69   BRUSH/BR/RUSTON/EMD   Co-Co

These locomotives are heavy rebuilds of Class 56s for GB Railfreight, with new General Motors engines, the same type as used in the Class 66s. The first rebuild were completed and entered service in 2021 and 16 locomotives will be rebuilt. Donor locomotives shown for 69011–017 are provisional.

Built: 1976–84 by Electroputere at Craiova, Romania (as sub-contractors for Brush) or BREL at Doncaster or Crewe Works. Rebuilt 2019–24 by ElectroMotive Diesel Services, Longport.
Engine: General Motors 12N-710G3B-T2 two stroke of 2385 kW (3200 hp) at 904 rpm.
Main Traction Alternator: General Motors EMD AR10/CA6.
Traction Motors: Brush TM73-62.
Maximum Tractive Effort: 280kN (62900 lbf).
Continuous Tractive Effort: 240kN (54000 lbf).

Power at Rail: 2080 kW.	**Train Brakes:** Air.
Brake Force: 60 tonnes.	**Dimensions:** 19.36 x 2.79 m.
Weight: 125 tonnes.	**Wheel Diameter:** 1143 mm.
Design Speed: 80 mph.	**Maximum Speed:** 80 mph.

Fuel Capacity: 5200 litres.
Train Supply: Not equipped.
Route Availability: 7.
Total: 16.

Non-standard livery: 69004 British Rail Railway Technical Centre (red & dark blue).

69001	(56031)	**GB**	PG	GBRG	TN	Mayflower
69002	(56311)	**BL**	PG	GBRG	TN	Bob Tiller CM&EE
69003	(56018)	**GB**	PG	GBRG	TN	The Railway Observer
69004	(56069)	**O**	PG	GBRG	TN	
69005	(56007)	**G**	PG	GBRG	TN	Eastleigh
69006	(56128)	**GB**	PG	GBRG	TN	Pathfinder Railtours Peter Watts 50 years service 1973–2023
69007	(56037)	**B**	PG	GBRG	TN	Richard Trevithick
69008	(56038)	**GB**	PG	GBRG	TN	
69009	(56060)		PG			
69010	(56065)	**U**	PG	GBRG	TN	
69011	(56032)		PG			
69012	(56077)		PG			
69013	(56312)		PG			
69014	(56104)		PG			
69015	(56009)		PG			
69016	(56097)		PG			

CLASS 70 GENERAL ELECTRIC Co-Co

GE "PowerHaul" locomotives. 70012 was badly damaged whilst being unloaded in 2011 and was returned to Pennsylvania.

70801 (built as 70099) is a Turkish-built demonstrator that arrived in Britain in 2012. Colas Rail leased this locomotive and then in 2013 ordered a further nine locomotives (70802–810) that were delivered in 2014. 70811–817 followed in 2017.

Built: 2009–17 by General Electric, Erie, Pennsylvania, USA or by TÜLOMSAS, Eskişehir, Turkey (70801).
Engine: General Electric PowerHaul P616LDA1 of 2848 kW (3820 hp) at 1500 rpm.
Main Alternator: General Electric GTA series.
Traction Motors: AC-GE 5GEB30.
Maximum Tractive Effort: 544 kN (122000 lbf).
Continuous Tractive Effort: 427 kN (96000 lbf) at 11 mph.
Power at Rail:
Brake Force: 96.7 t.
Weight: 129 t.
Design Speed: 75 mph.
Fuel Capacity: 6000 litres.
Train Supply: Not equipped.
Train Brakes: Air.
Dimensions: 21.71 x 2.64 m.
Wheel Diameter: 1066 mm.
Maximum Speed: 75 mph.
Route Availability: 7.
Total: 36.

Class 70/0. Freightliner locomotives.

70001	**FH**	AK	DFGI	LD	PowerHaul
70002	**FH**	AK	DFGI	LD	
70003	**FH**	AK	DFGI	LD	
70004	**FH**	AK	DFGI	LD	The Coal Industry Society
70005	**FH**	AK	DFGI	LD	
70006	**FH**	AK	DFGI	LD	
70007	**FH**	AK	DFGI	LD	
70008	**FH**	AK	DFGI	LD	
70009	**FH**	AK	DHLT	LD (S)	
70010	**FH**	AK	DFGI	LD	
70011	**FH**	AK	DFGI	LD	
70013	**FH**	AK	DHLT	LD (S)	
70014	**FH**	AK	DFGI	LD	
70015	**FH**	AK	DFGI	LD	
70016	**FH**	AK	DFGI	LD	
70017	**FH**	AK	DFGI	LD	
70018	**FH**	AK	DHLT	LD (S)	
70019	**FH**	AK	DHLT	LD (S)	
70020	**FH**	AK	DFGI	LD	

Class 70/8. Colas Rail locomotives.

70801	**CS**	LF	COLO	CF
70802	**CS**	LF	COLO	CF
70803	**CS**	LF	COLO	CF
70804	**CS**	LF	COLO	CF
70805	**CS**	LF	COLO	CF
70806	**CS**	LF	COLO	CF
70807	**CS**	LF	COLO	CF
70808	**CS**	LF	COLO	CF
70809	**CS**	LF	COLO	CF
70810	**CS**	LF	COLO	CF
70811	**CS**	BN	COLO	CF
70812	**CS**	BN	COLO	CF
70813	**CS**	BN	COLO	CF
70814	**CS**	BN	COLO	CF
70815	**CS**	BN	COLO	CF
70816	**CS**	BN	COLO	CF
70817	**CS**	BN	COLO	CF

2. ELECTRO-DIESEL & ELECTRIC LOCOMOTIVES

CLASS 73/1   BR/ENGLISH ELECTRIC   Bo-Bo

Electro-diesel locomotives which can operate either from a DC supply or using power from a diesel engine.

Built: 1965–67 by English Electric Co. at Vulcan Foundry, Newton-le-Willows.
Engine: English Electric 4SRKT of 447 kW (600 hp) at 850 rpm.
Main Generator: English Electric 824/5D.
Electric Supply System: 750 V DC from third rail.
Traction Motors: English Electric 546/1B.
Maximum Tractive Effort (Electric): 179 kN (40000 lbf).
Maximum Tractive Effort (Diesel): 160 kN (36000 lbf).
Continuous Rating (Electric): 1060 kW (1420 hp) giving a tractive effort of 35 kN (7800 lbf) at 68 mph.
Continuous Tractive Effort (Diesel): 60 kN (13600 lbf) at 11.5 mph.
Maximum Rail Power (Electric): 2350 kW (3150 hp) at 42 mph.
Train Brakes: Air, vacuum & electro-pneumatic († Air & electro-pneumatic).
Brake Force: 31 t.   **Dimensions:** 16.36 x 2.64 m.
Weight: 77 t.   **Wheel Diameter:** 1016 mm.
Design Speed: 90 mph.   **Maximum Speed:** 90 mph.
Fuel Capacity: 1409 litres.   **Route Availability:** 6.
Train Supply: Electric, index 66 (on electric power only). **Total:** 15.

Formerly numbered E6007–E6020/E6022–E6026/E6028–E6049 (not in order).

Locomotives numbered in the 732xx series are classed as 73/2 and were originally dedicated to Gatwick Express services.

There have been two separate Class 73 rebuild projects. For GBRf 11 locomotives were rebuilt at Brush, Loughborough with a 1600 hp MTU engine (renumbered 73961–971). For Network Rail 73104/211 were rebuilt at RVEL Derby (now LORAM) with 2 x QSK19 750 hp engines (73951/952).

Non-standard liveries and numbering:

73110   Carries original number E6016.
73139   Light blue & light grey.
73235   Plain dark blue.

73101	**PC**	GB	GBZZ	ZG (S)	
73107	**GB**	GB	GBED	SE	Tracy
73109	**GB**	GB	GBED	SE	Battle of Britain 80th Anniversary
73110	**B**	GB	GBZZ	ZG (S)	
73119	**CE**	GB	GBED	SE	Paul Taylor
73128	**GB**	GB	GBED	SE	O.V.S. BULLEID C.B.E.
73136	**GB**	GB	GBED	SE	Mhairi
73138	**Y**	NR	QADD	RO (S)	
73139	**O**	GB	GBZZ	ZG (S)	

73141	**GB**	GB	GBED	SE	SPA VALLEY RAILWAY 25 YEAR ANNIVERSARY
73201 †	**B**	GB	GBED	SE	Broadlands
73202 †	**SN**	GB	GBED	SE	
73212 †	**GB**	GB	GBED	SE	Stephen Eaves
73213 †	**GB**	GB	GBED	SE	Rhodalyn
73235 †	**O**	P	HYWD	BM	

CLASS 73/9 (RVEL)   BR/RVEL   Bo-Bo

The 7395x number series was used for rebuilt Network Rail locomotives.

Rebuilt: Re-engineered by RVEL Derby 2013–15.
Engine: 2 x QSK19 of 560 kW (750 hp) at 1800 rpm (total 1120 kw (1500 hp)).
Main Alternator: 2 x Marathon Magnaplus.
Electric Supply System: 750 V DC from third rail.
Traction Motors: English Electric 546/1B.
Maximum Tractive Effort (Electric): 179 kN (40000 lbf).
Maximum Tractive Effort (Diesel): 179 kN (40000 lbf).
Continuous Rating (Electric): 1060 kW (1420 hp) giving a tractive effort of 35 kN (7800 lbf) at 68 mph.
Continuous Tractive Effort (Diesel): 990 kW (1328 hp) giving a tractive effort of 33 kN (7420 lbf) at 68 mph.
Maximum Rail Power (Electric): 2350 kW (3150 hp) at 42 mph.

Train Brakes: Air.	**Brake Force:** 31 t.
Weight: 77 t.	**Dimensions:** 16.36 x 2.64 m.
Maximum Speed: 90 mph.	**Wheel Diameter:** 1016 mm.
Fuel Capacity: 2260 litres.	**Route Availability:** 6.
Train Supply: Not equipped.	**Total:** 2.

73951	(73104)	**Y**	LO	QADD	KR (S)	Malcolm Brinded
73952	(73211)	**Y**	LO	QADD	KR (S)	Janis Kong

CLASS 73/9 (GBRf)   BR/BRUSH   Bo-Bo

GBRf Class 73s rebuilt at Brush Loughborough. 73961–965 are normally used on Network Rail contracts and 73966–971 are used by Caledonian Sleeper.

Rebuilt: Re-engineered by Brush, Loughborough 2014–16.
Engine: MTU 8V4000 R43L of 1195 kW (1600 hp) at 1800 rpm.
Main Alternator: Lechmotoren SDV 87.53-12.
Electric Supply System: 750 V DC from third rail (73961–965 only).
Traction Motors: English Electric 546/1B.
Maximum Tractive Effort (Electric): 179 kN (40000 lbf).
Maximum Tractive Effort (Diesel): 179 kN (40000 lbf).
Continuous Rating (Electric): 1060 kW (1420 hp) giving a tractive effort of 35 kN (7800 lbf) at 68 mph.
Continuous Tractive Effort (Diesel):
Maximum Rail Power (Electric): 2350 kW (3150 hp) at 42 mph.

Train Brakes: Air.	**Brake Force:** 31 t.
Weight: 77 t.	**Dimensions:** 16.36 x 2.64 m.
Maximum Speed: 90 mph.	**Wheel Diameter:** 1016 mm.

Fuel Capacity: 1409 litres.   **Route Availability:** 6.
Train Supply: Electric, index 38 (electric & diesel). **Total:** 11.

73961	(73209)	**GB** GB	GBNR	SE	Alison
73962	(73204)	**GB** GB	GBNR	SE	Dick Mabbutt
73963	(73206)	**GB** GB	GBNR	SE	Janice
73964	(73205)	**GB** GB	GBNR	SE	Jeanette
73965	(73208)	**GB** GB	GBNR	SE	Des O' Brien

73966–971 have been rebuilt for Caledonian Sleeper but their third rail electric capability has been retained. They have a higher Train Supply index and a slightly higher fuel capacity. Details as 73961–965 except:
Fuel Capacity: 1509 litres.   **Train Supply:** Electric, index 96.

73005 and 73006 were originally assembled at Eastleigh Works.

73966	(73005)	d **CA** GB	GBCS	EC
73967	(73006)	d **CA** GB	GBCS	EC
73968	(73117)	d **CA** GB	GBCS	EC
73969	(73105)	d **CA** GB	GBCS	EC
73970	(73103)	d **CA** GB	GBCS	EC
73971	(73207)	d **CA** GB	GBCS	EC

CLASS 86   BR/ENGLISH ELECTRIC   Bo-Bo

Built: 1965–66 by English Electric Co at Vulcan Foundry, Newton-le-Willows or by BR at Doncaster Works.
Electric Supply System: 25 kV AC 50 Hz overhead.
Traction Motors: AEI 282BZ axle hung.
Maximum Tractive Effort: 207 kN (46500 lbf).
Continuous Rating: 3010 kW (4040 hp) giving a tractive effort of 85 kN (19200 lbf) at 77.5 mph.
Maximum Rail Power: 4550 kW (6100 hp) at 49.5 mph.

Train Brakes: Air.	**Brake Force:** 40 t.
Dimensions: 17.83 x 2.65 m.	**Weight:** 83–86.8 t.
Wheel Diameter: 1156 mm.	**Train Supply:** Electric, index 74.
Design Speed: 110–125 mph.	**Maximum Speed:** 100 mph.
Route Availability: 6.	**Total:** 3.

Formerly numbered E3101–E3200 (not in order).

Class 86s exported for use abroad are listed in section 5 of this book.

Class 86/1. Class 87-type bogies & motors. Details as above except:

Traction Motors: GEC 412AZ frame mounted.
Maximum Tractive Effort: 258 kN (58000 lbf).
Continuous Rating: 3730 kW (5000 hp) giving a tractive effort of 95 kN (21300 lbf) at 87 mph.
Maximum Rail Power: 5860 kW (7860 hp) at 50.8 mph.
Wheel Diameter: 1150 mm.
Design Speed: 110 mph.   **Maximum Speed:** 110 mph.

86101	**IC**	LS	LSLO	CL	Sir William A Stanier FRS

Class 86/2. Standard design rebuilt with resilient wheels & Flexicoil suspension. Details as in main class heading.

Non-standard livery: BR "Electric blue". Also carries number E3137.

86259 x   **0**   PP   MBEL   RU   Les Ross/Peter Pan

Class 86/4. Details as Class 86/2 except:

Traction Motors: AEI 282AZ axle hung.
Maximum Tractive Effort: 258 kN (58000 lbf).
Continuous Rating: 2680 kW (3600 hp) giving a tractive effort of 89 kN (20000 lbf) at 67 mph.
Maximum Rail Power: 4400 kW (5900 hp) at 38 mph.
Weight: 83–83.9 t.
Design Speed: 100 mph.   **Maximum Speed:** 100 mph.

86401   **CA**   WC   AWCA   CS   Mons Meg

CLASS 87   BREL/GEC   Bo-Bo

Built: 1973–75 by BREL at Crewe Works.
Electric Supply System: 25 kV AC 50 Hz overhead.
Traction Motors: GEC G412AZ frame mounted.
Maximum Tractive Effort: 258 kN (58000 lbf).
Continuous Rating: 3730 kW (5000 hp) giving a tractive effort of 95 kN (21300 lbf) at 87 mph.
Maximum Rail Power: 5860 kW (7860 hp) at 50.8 mph.
Train Brakes: Air.   **Brake Force:** 40 t.
Dimensions: 17.83 x 2.65 m.   **Weight:** 83.3 t.
Wheel Diameter: 1150 mm.   **Train Supply:** Electric, index 95.
Design Speed: 110 mph.   **Maximum Speed:** 110 mph.
Route Availability: 6.   **Total:** 1.

Class 87s exported for use abroad are listed in section 5 of this book.

87002   **IC**   LS   LSLO   CL   Royal Sovereign

CLASS 88   VOSSLOH/STADLER   Bo-Bo

Vossloh/Stadler bi-mode DRS locomotives.

Built: 2015–16 by Vossloh/Stadler, Valencia, Spain.
Electric Supply System: 25 kV AC 50 Hz overhead.
Engine: Caterpillar C27 12-cylinder of 708 kW (950 hp) at 1750 rpm.
Main Alternator: ABB AMXL400.
Traction Motors: ABB AMXL400.
Maximum Tractive Effort (Electric): 317 kN (71260 lbf).
Maximum Tractive Effort (Diesel): 317 kN (71260 lbf).
Continuous Rating: 4000 kW (5360 hp) giving a tractive effort of 258 kN (58000 lbf) at 28 mph (electric).
Maximum Rail Power:

Train Brakes: Air, regenerative & rheostatic.
Brake Force: 73 t.
Weight: 85 t.
Fuel Capacity: 1800 litres.
Design Speed: 100 mph.
Route Availability: 7.

Dimensions: 20.50 x 2.69 m.
Wheel Diameter: 1100 mm.
Train Supply: Electric, index 96.
Maximum Speed: 100 mph.
Total: 10.

Non-standard livery: 88010 Refrigerated rail COOL move (blue & white).

88001	**DI**	BN	XHVE	KM	Revolution
88002	**DI**	BN	XHVE	KM	Prometheus
88003	**DI**	BN	XHVE	KM	Genesis
88004	**DI**	BN	XHVE	KM	Pandora
88005	**DI**	BN	XHVE	KM	Minerva
88006	**DI**	BN	XHVE	KM	Juno
88007	**DI**	BN	XHVE	KM	Electra
88008	**DI**	BN	XHVE	KM	Ariadne
88009	**DI**	BN	XHVE	KM	Diana
88010	**O**	BN	XHVE	KM	Aurora

CLASS 90   GEC   Bo-Bo

Built: 1987–90 by BREL at Crewe Works (as sub-contractors for GEC).
Electric Supply System: 25 kV AC 50 Hz overhead.
Traction Motors: GEC G412CY frame mounted.
Maximum Tractive Effort: 258 kN (58000 lbf).
Continuous Rating: 3730 kW (5000 hp) giving a tractive effort of 95 kN (21300 lbf) at 87 mph.
Maximum Rail Power: 5860 kW (7860 hp) at 68.3 mph.
Train Brakes: Air.
Brake Force: 40 t.
Weight: 84.5 t.
Design Speed: 110 mph.
Train Supply: Electric, index 95.

Dimensions: 18.80 x 2.74 m.
Wheel Diameter: 1150 mm.
Maximum Speed: 110 mph.
Route Availability: 7.
Total: 50.

Advertising liveries:

90021   Malcolm Group – 100 Years (blue & black).
90024   Malcolm Logistics (blue).
90039   I am the backbone of the economy (black).

90001	b	**IC**	LS	LSLO	CL	Royal Scot
90002	b	**IC**	LS	LSLO	CL	Wolf of Badenoch
90003		**FG**	FL	DFLC	CB	
90004		**FG**	FL	DFLC	CB	
90005		**FG**	FL	DFLC	CB	
90006		**FG**	FL	DFLC	CB	Modern Railways Magazine/ Roger Ford
90007		**FG**	FL	DFLC	CB	
90008		**FG**	FL	DFLC	CB	
90009		**FG**	FL	DFLC	CB	
90010		**FG**	FL	DFLC	CB	

90011	**FG**	FL	DFLC	CB	
90012	**FG**	FL	DFLC	CB	
90013	**FG**	FL	DFLC	CB	
90014	**FG**	FL	DFLC	CB	Over the Rainbow
90015	**FG**	FL	DFLC	CB	
90016	**FG**	FL	DFLC	CB	
90017	**E**	DB	WQDA	CE (S)	
90018	**DB**	DB	WQDA	CE (S)	The Pride of Bellshill
90019	**DB**	DB	WQDA	CE (S)	Multimodal
90020	**GC**	DB	WQBA	CE (S)	
90021	**AL**	DB	WQBA	CE (S)	Donald Malcolm
90022	**EG**	DB	WQBA	CE (S)	Freightconnection
90023	**E**	DB	WQDA	CE (S)	
90024	**AL**	DB	WQBA	CE (S)	
90025	**F**	DB	WQDA	CE (S)	
90026	**GC**	DB	WQBA	CE (S)	
90027	**F**	DB	WQDA	CE (S)	Allerton T&RS Depot
90028	**DB**	DB	WQBA	CE (S)	Sir William McAlpine
90029	**GC**	DB	WQBA	CE (S)	
90030	**E**	DB	WQDA	CE (S)	
90031	**E**	DB	WQDA	CE (S)	The Railway Children Partnership Working For Street Children Worldwide
90032	**E**	DB	WQDA	CE (S)	
90033	**FE**	DB	WQDA	CE (S)	
90034	**DR**	DB	WQBA	CE (S)	
90035	**DB**	DB	WQDA	CE (S)	
90036	**DB**	DB	WQBA	CE (S)	Driver Jack Mills
90037	**DB**	DB	WQBA	CE (S)	Christine
90038	**FE**	DB	WQDA	CE (S)	
90039	**AL**	DB	WQBA	CE (S)	The Chartered Institute of Logistics and Transport
90040	**DB**	DB	WQDA	CE (S)	
90041	**FG**	FL	DFLC	CB	
90042	**FH**	FL	DFLC	CB	
90043	**FH**	FL	DFLC	CB	
90044	**FG**	FL	DFLC	CB	
90045	**FH**	FL	DFLC	CB	
90046	**FL**	FL	DFLC	CB	
90047	**FG**	FL	DFLC	CB	
90048	**FG**	FL	DFLC	CB	
90049	**FH**	FL	DFLC	CB	
90050	**FF**	AV	DHLT	CQ (S)	

CLASS 91   GEC   Bo-Bo

Built: 1988–91 by BREL at Crewe Works (as sub-contractors for GEC).
Electric Supply System: 25 kV AC 50 Hz overhead.
Traction Motors: GEC G426AZ.
Maximum Tractive Effort: 190 kN (43 000 lbf).
Continuous Rating: 4540 kW (6090 hp) giving a tractive effort of 170 kN at 46 mph.
Maximum Rail Power: 4700 kW (6300 hp) at ?? mph.

Train Brakes: Air.	**Dimensions:** 19.41 x 2.74 m.
Brake Force: 45 t.	**Wheel Diameter:** 1000 mm.
Weight: 84 t.	**Maximum Speed:** 125 mph.
Design Speed: 140 mph.	**Route Availability:** 7.
Train Supply: Electric, index 95.	**Total:** 14.

Locomotives were originally numbered in the 910xx series, but were renumbered upon completion of overhauls at Bombardier, Doncaster by the addition of 100 to their original number.

Advertising liveries:

91110   Battle of Britain (black and grey).
91111   For the fallen (various with poppy and Union Jack vinyls).

91101	**LC**	E	IECA	NL	FLYING SCOTSMAN
91105	**LC**	E	IECA	NL	
91106	**LC**	E	IECA	NL	
91107	**LC**	E	IECA	NL	SKYFALL
91109	**LC**	E	IECA	NL	Sir Bobby Robson
91110	**AL**	E	IECA	NL	BATTLE OF BRITAIN MEMORIAL FLIGHT
91111	**AL**	E	IECA	NL	For the Fallen
91114	**LC**	E	IECA	NL	Durham Cathedral
91117	**EX**	EP	EPUK	BH (S)	
91119	**IC**	E	IECA	NL	Bounds Green INTERCITY Depot 1977–2017
91120	**IC**	EP	EPUK	CQ	
91124	**LC**	E	IECA	NL	
91127	**LC**	E	IECA	NL	Neville Hill
91130	**LC**	E	IECA	NL	Lord Mayor of Newcastle

CLASS 92   BRUSH   Co-Co

Built: 1993–96 by Brush Traction at Loughborough.
Electric Supply System: 25 kV AC 50 Hz overhead or 750 V DC third rail.
Traction Motors: Asea Brown Boveri design. Model 6FRA 7059B Asynchronous 3-phase induction motors).
Maximum Tractive Effort: 400 kN (90 000 lbf).
Continuous Rating: 5040 kW (6760 hp) on AC, 4000 kW (5360 hp) on DC.
Maximum Rail Power: 5040 kW (6760 hp) on AC, 4000 kW (5360 hp) on DC.

Maximum Rail Power:	**Train Brakes:** Air.
Brake Force: 63 t.	**Dimensions:** 21.34 x 2.67 m.
Weight: 126 t.	**Wheel Diameter:** 1070 mm.
Design Speed: 140 km/h (87 mph).	**Maximum Speed:** 140 km/h (87 mph).

Train Supply: Electric, index 180 (AC), 108 (DC).
Route Availability: 7.   **Total:** 33.

* Fitted with TVM430 signalling equipment to operate on High Speed 1.

Class 92s exported for use abroad are listed in section 1.6 of this book.

Advertising livery: 92017 Stobart Rail (two-tone blue & white).

92004	**EG**	DB	WQCA	CE (S)	Jane Austen
92006	d **CA**	GB	GBSL	WB	
92007	**EG**	DB	WQBA	CE (S)	Schubert
92008	**EG**	DB	WQCA	CE (S)	Jules Verne
92009	* **DB**	DB	WFAC	CE	Marco Polo
92010	*d **CA**	GB	GBSL	WB	
92011	* **EG**	DB	WFBC	CE	Handel
92013	**EG**	DB	WQBA	CE (S)	Puccini
92014	d **CA**	GB	GBSL	WB	
92015	* **DB**	DB	WFBC	CE	
92016	* **DB**	DB	WQCA	CE (S)	
92017	**AL**	DB	WQCA	CE (S)	Bart the Engine
92018	*d **CA**	GB	GBST	WB	
92019	* **EG**	DB	WFBC	CE	Wagner
92020	d **GB**	GB	GBSL	WB	BILLY STIRLING
92021	**EP**	GB	GBSD	WS (S)	Purcell
92023	*d **CA**	GB	GBSL	WB	
92028	d **GB**	GB	GBST	WB	
92029	**DB**	DB	WFAC	CE	
92031	* **DB**	DB	WQBA	CE (S)	
92032	*d **GB**	GB	GBCT	WB	IMechE Railway Division
92033	d **CA**	GB	GBSL	WB	Railway Heritage Trust
92035	**EG**	DB	WQCA	CE (S)	Mendelssohn
92036	* **EG**	DB	WFBC	CE	Bertolt Brecht
92037	**EG**	DB	WQCA	CE (S)	Sullivan
92038	*d **CA**	GB	GBST	WB	
92040	**EP**	GB	GBSD	WS (S)	Goethe
92041	* **EG**	DB	WFBC	CE	Vaughan Williams
92042	* **DB**	DB	WFBC	CE	
92043	*d **GB**	GB	GBST	WB	Andy Withers 50 YEARS SERVICE
92044	* **EP**	GB	GBCT	WB	Couperin
92045	**EP**	GB	GBSD	WS (S)	Chaucer
92046	**EP**	GB	GBSD	WS (S)	Sweelinck

CLASS 93   STADLER   Bo-Bo

In January 2021 Rail Operations Group placed a order with Stadler for a
new design of mixed-traffic tri-mode locomotives, designated Class 93. The
framework order is for an initial 30 locomotives, to be confirmed in batches
of ten.

The locomotive is a development of the DRS Class 88 and as well as having
a more powerful CAT diesel engine and electric capability will be fitted with

batteries and a higher maximum speed of 110 mph. The first locomotive was delivered in June 2023. Full details awaited.

Built: 2021–24 by Stadler, Valencia, Spain.
Electric Supply System: 25 kV AC 50 Hz overhead.
Engine: Caterpillar C32 12-cylinder of 900 kW (1205 hp) at   rpm.
Batteries: 2 x LTO battery packs providing 400 kW (535 hp).
Main Alternator:
Traction Motors:
Maximum Tractive Effort: 290 kN (65200 lbf).
Continuous Rating: 4660 kW (5360 hp).
Maximum Rail Power:
Train Brakes: Air, regenerative & electro-pneumatic.
Brake Force: 73 t.
Weight: 86 t.
Fuel Capacity: 3600 litres.
Design Speed: 110 mph.
Route Availability: 7.

Dimensions:
Wheel Diameter:
Train Supply:
Maximum Speed: 110 mph.
Total: 30.

93001	**RG**	RO
93002	**RG**	RO
93003		RO
93004		RO
93005		RO
93006		RO
93007		RO
93008		RO
93009		RO
93010		RO
93011		RO
93012		RO
93013		RO
93014		RO
93015		RO
93016		RO
93017		RO
93018		RO
93019		RO
93020		RO
93021		RO
93022		RO
93023		RO
93024		RO
93025		RO
93026		RO
93027		RO
93028		RO
93029		RO
93030		RO

CLASS 99   STADLER EURODUAL   Co-Co

In April 2022 GB Railfreight placed a order with Stadler for 30 of a British version of Stadler's Eurodual design, to be designated Class 99.

The locomotive is principally designed for heavy freight duties and is bi-mode, operating off either 25 kV AC overhead electrification or an onboard diesel engine. 30 have been ordered with an option for a further 20. The first locomotives are due to enter service in 2025. Full details awaited.

Built: 2023– by Stadler, Valencia, Spain.
Electric Supply System: 25 kV AC 50 Hz overhead.
Engine: 1.8 Mw Cummins QSK50.
Main Alternator:
Traction Motors:
Maximum Tractive Effort (Electric): 500 kN (112 400 lbf).
Maximum Tractive Effort (Diesel):
Continuous Rating: 6000 kW (8000 hp).
Maximum Rail Power:
Train Brakes: Air, regenerative & electro-pneumatic.

Brake Force:	**Dimensions:**
Weight:	**Wheel Diameter:**
Fuel Capacity: 3000 litres.	**Train Supply:**
Design Speed: 75 mph.	**Maximum Speed:** 75 mph.
Route Availability:	**Total:** 30.

99001	BN
99002	BN
99003	BN
99004	BN
99005	BN
99006	BN
99007	BN
99008	BN
99009	BN
99010	BN
99011	BN
99012	BN
99013	BN
99014	BN
99015	BN
99016	BN
99017	BN
99018	BN
99019	BN
99020	BN
99021	BN
99022	BN
99023	BN
99024	BN
99025	BN
99026	BN

99027	BN
99028	BN
99029	BN
99030	BN

3. EUROTUNNEL LOCOMOTIVES

DIESEL LOCOMOTIVES

0001–10 are registered on TOPS as 21901–910.

0001–0005   Krupp MaK   Bo-Bo

Channel Tunnel maintenance and rescue train locomotives.
Built: 1991–92 by MaK at Kiel, Germany (Model DE 1004).
Engine: MTU 12V396 TC 13 of 950 kW (1275 hp) at 1800 rpm.
Main Alternator: ABB.   **Traction Motors:** ABB.
Maximum Tractive Effort: 305 kN (68600 lbf).
Continuous Tractive Effort: 140 kN (31500 lbf) at 20 mph.
Power At Rail: 750 kW (1012 hp).   **Dimensions:** 14.40 x ?? m.
Brake Force: 120 kN.   **Wheel Diameter:** 1000 mm.
Train Brakes: Air.   **Weight:** 90 t.
Maximum Speed: 100 km/h.   **Design Speed:** 120 km/h.
Fuel Capacity: 3500 litres.   **Multiple Working:** Within class.
Train Supply: Not equipped.   **Signalling System:** TVM430 cab signalling.

0001	**GY**	ET	CT		0004	**GY**	ET	CT
0002	**GY**	ET	CT		0005	**GY**	ET	CT
0003	**GY**	ET	CT				

0006–0010   Krupp MaK   Bo-Bo

Channel Tunnel maintenance and rescue locomotives. Rebuilt from Netherlands Railways/DB Cargo Nederland Class 6400. 0006/07 were added to the Eurotunnel fleet in 2011, and 0008–10 in 2016.

Built: 1990–91 by MaK at Kiel, Germany (Model DE 6400).
Engine: MTU 12V396 TC 13 of 1180 kW (1580 hp) at 1800 rpm.
Main Alternator: ABB.   **Traction Motors:** ABB.
Maximum Tractive Effort: 290 kN (65200 lbf).
Continuous Tractive Effort: 140 kN (31500 lbf) at 20 mph.
Power At Rail: 750 kW (1012 hp).   **Dimensions:** 14.40 x ?? m.
Brake Force: 120 kN.   **Wheel Diameter:** 1000 mm.
Train Brakes: Air.   **Weight:** 80 t.
Maximum Speed: 120 km/h.   **Design Speed:** 120 km/h.
Fuel Capacity: 2900 litres.   **Multiple Working:** Within class.
Train Supply: Not equipped.

Not fitted with TVM 430 cab signalling so have to operate with another locomotive when used on HS1. 0010 can only be used for shunting at Coquelles depot.

0006	(6456)	**GY**	ET	CT		0009	(6451)	**GY**	ET	CT
0007	(6457)	**GY**	ET	CT		0010	(6447)	**EB**	ET	CO
0008	(6450)	**GY**	ET	CT						

0031–0042   HUNSLET/SCHÖMA   0-4-0

Built: 1989–90 by Hunslet Engine Company at Leeds as 900 mm gauge.
Rebuilt: 1993–94 by Schöma in Germany to 1435 mm gauge as Type CFL 200 DCL-R.
Engine: Deutz F10L 413 FW of 170 kW (230 hp) at 2300 rpm.
Transmission: Mechanical Clark 5421-179 type.
Maximum Tractive Effort: 68 kN (15300 lbf).
Continuous Tractive Effort: 47 kN (10570 lbf) at 5 mph.
Power At Rail: 130.1 kW (175 hp).
Brake Force: **Dimensions:** 7.87 (* 10.94) x 2.69 m.
Weight: 25 t. (* 28 t.)   **Wheel Diameter:** 1010 mm.
Maximum Speed: 48 km/h (* 75 km/h).
Fuel Capacity: 450 litres.   **Train Brakes:** Air.
Train Supply: Not equipped.   **Multiple Working:** Not equipped.

* Rebuilt with inspection platforms to check overhead catenary (Type CS 200).

0031		**GY**	ET	CT	FRANCES
0032		**GY**	ET	CT	ELISABETH
0033		**GY**	ET	CT	SILKE
0034		**GY**	ET	CT	AMANDA
0035		**GY**	ET	CT	MARY
0036		**GY**	ET	CT	LAURENCE
0037		**GY**	ET	CT	LYDIE
0038		**GY**	ET	CT	JENNY
0039	*	**GY**	ET	CT	PACITA
0040		**GY**	ET	CT	JILL
0041	*	**GY**	ET	CT	KIM
0042		**GY**	ET	CT	NICOLE

ELECTRIC LOCOMOTIVES

9005–9840   BRUSH/ABB   Bo-Bo-Bo

Built: 1993–2002 by Brush Traction, Loughborough.
Electric Supply System: 25 kV AC 50 Hz overhead.
Traction Motors: Asea Brown Boveri design. Asynchronous 3-phase motors Model 6FHA 7059 (as built). Model 6FHA 7059C (7000 kW rated locos).
Maximum Tractive Effort: 400kN (90 000 lbf).
Continuous Rating: Class 9/0: 5760 kW (7725 hp). Class 9/7 and 9/8: 7000 kW (9387 hp).

Maximum Rail Power:
Brake Force: 50 t.
Weight: 136 t.
Maximum Speed: 140 km/h.
Train Supply: Electric.

Multiple Working: TDM system.
Dimensions: 22.01 x 2.97 x 4.20 m.
Wheel Diameter: 1250 mm.
Design Speed: 140 km/h.
Train Brakes: Air.

Class 9/0 Original build locos. Built 1993–94.

9005	**EB**	ET	CO	JESSYE NORMAN
9007	**EB**	ET	CO	
9011	**EB**	ET	CO	JOSÉ VAN DAM[1]
9013	**EB**	ET	CO	MARIA CALLAS[1]
9015	**EB**	ET	CO	LÖTSCHBERG 1913[1]
9018	**EB**	ET	CO	WILHELMENIA FERNANDEZ
9022	**EB**	ET	CO	DAME JANET BAKER
9024	**EB**	ET	CO	GOTTHARD 1882
9026	**EB**	ET	CO	
9029	**EB**	ET	CO	THOMAS ALLEN
9033	**EB**	ET	CO	MONTSERRAT CABALLE
9036	**EB**	ET	CO	ALAIN FONDARY[1]
9037	**EB**	ET	CO	

Class 9/7. Increased power freight shuttle locos. Built 2001–02 (9711–23 built 1998–2001 as 9101–13 and rebuilt as 9711–23 2010–12).

9701	**EB**	ET	CO	
9702	**EB**	ET	CO	
9703	**EB**	ET	CO	
9704	**EB**	ET	CO	
9705	**EB**	ET	CO	
9706	**EB**	ET	CO	
9707	**EB**	ET	CO	

9711	(9101)	**EB**	ET	CO
9712	(9102)	**EB**	ET	CO
9713	(9103)	**EB**	ET	CO
9714	(9104)	**EB**	ET	CO
9715	(9105)	**EB**	ET	CO
9716	(9106)	**EB**	ET	CO
9717	(9107)	**EB**	ET	CO
9718	(9108)	**EB**	ET	CO
9719	(9109)	**EB**	ET	CO
9720	(9110)	**EB**	ET	CO
9721	(9111)	**EB**	ET	CO
9722	(9112)	**EB**	ET	CO
9723	(9113)	**EB**	ET	CO

Class 9/8 Locos rebuilt from Class 9/0 by adding 800 to the loco number. Uprated to 7000 kW.

90xx and 98xx locomotives have a cab in the blunt end for shunting, except 9840 which does not have this feature.

9801	**EB**	ET	CO	LESLEY GARRETT
9802	**EB**	ET	CO	STUART BURROWS

9803	**EB**	ET	CO	BENJAMIN LUXON[1]
9804	**EB**	ET	CO	
9806	**EB**	ET	CO	REGINE CRESPIN
9808	**EB**	ET	CO	ELISABETH SODERSTROM
9809	**EB**	ET	CO	
9810	**EB**	ET	CO	
9812	**EB**	ET	CO	LUCIANO PAVAROTTI[1]
9814	**EB**	ET	CO	LUCIA POPP
9816	**EB**	ET	CO	
9819	**EB**	ET	CO	MARIA EWING[1]
9820	**EB**	ET	CO	NICOLAI GHIAROV
9821	**EB**	ET	CO	
9823	**EB**	ET	CO	DAME ELISABETH LEGGE-SCHWARZKOPF
9825	**EB**	ET	CO	
9827	**EB**	ET	CO	BARBARA HENDRICKS
9828	**EB**	ET	CO	DAME KIRI TE KANAWA[1]
9831	**EB**	ET	CO	
9832	**EB**	ET	CO	RENATA TEBALDI[1]
9834	**EB**	ET	CO	MIRELLA FRENI
9835	**EB**	ET	CO	NICOLAI GEDDA
9838	**EB**	ET	CO	HILDEGARD BEHRENS
9840	**EB**	ET	CO	

[1] nameplates carried on one side only.

4. LOCOMOTIVES AWAITING DISPOSAL

Locomotives that are still extant but best classed as awaiting disposal are listed here.

66048   EMD, Longport Works

5. LOCOMOTIVES EXPORTED FOR USE ABROAD

This section details former British Railways (plus privatisation era) diesel and electric locomotives that have been exported from Great Britain for use in industrial locations or with a main line operator abroad. Not included are locos that are classed as "preserved" abroad. These can be found in the Platform 5 "Preserved Locomotives of British Railways" publication.

(S) denotes locomotives that are stored.

Number Other no./name   *Operator/Location*

Class 03

03156		Ferramenta Pugliese, Terlizzi, Bari, Italy

Class 43

43022		Ferrocarril del Istmo de Tehuantepec, Mexico
43158		Ferrocarril del Istmo de Tehuantepec, Mexico
43170		Ferrocarril del Istmo de Tehuantepec, Mexico

Class 47

47375	92 70 00 47375-5	Komplex Rail, Hungary

Class 56

56101	92 55 0659 001-5	V-Híd, Hungary
56115	92 55 0659 002-3	V-Híd, Hungary
56117	92 55 0659 003-1	V-Híd, Hungary (S) Budapest Keleti

Class 58

58025		DB, Spain, (S) Albacete
58027	L52	DB, Spain, (S) Albacete
58041	L36	Transfesa, Spain, (S) Albacete
58044		DB, France, (S) Woippy, Metz
58050	L53	DB, Spain, (S) Albacete

Class 66

The second number shown is the running number for the locomotives operated by Freightliner in Poland.

66022	DBC, France	66064	DBC, France	66173	DBC, Poland
66029	DBC, France	66071	DBC, France	66178	DBC, Poland
66033	DBC, France	66072	DBC, France	66180	DBC, Poland
66036	DBC, France	66123	DBC, France	66189	DBC, Poland
66038	DBC, France	66146	DBC, Poland	66191	DBC, France
66042	DBC, France	66153	DBC, Poland	66193	DBC, France
66045	DBC, France	66157	DBC, Poland	66195	DBC, France
66049	DBC, France	66159	DBC, Poland	66196	DBC, Poland
66052	DBC, France	66163	DBC, Poland	66201	DBC, France
66062	DBC, France	66166	DBC, Poland	66202	DBC, France

66203	DBC, Poland	66227	DBC, Poland	66249		DBC, France
66204	DBC, Poland	66228	DBC, France	66411	66013	FL, Poland
66208	DBC, France	66229	DBC, France	66412	66015	FL, Poland
66209	DBC, France	66231	DBC, France	66417	66014	FL, Poland
66210	DBC, France	66232	DBC, France	66527	66016	FL, Poland
66211	DBC, France	66233	DBC, France	66530	66017	FL, Poland
66212	DBC, France	66234	DBC, France	66535	66018	FL, Poland
66213	DBC, France	66235	DBC, France	66582	66009	FL, Poland
66214	DBC, France	66236	DBC, France	66583	66010	FL, Poland
66215	DBC, France	66237	DBC, Poland	66584	66011	FL, Poland
66216	DBC, France	66239	DBC, France	66586	66008	FL, Poland
66217	DBC, France	66240	DBC, France	66595	66020	FL, Poland
66218	DBC, France	66241	DBC, France	66608	66603	FL, Poland
66219	DBC, France	66242	DBC, France	66609	66605	FL, Poland
66220	DBC, Poland	66243	DBC, France	66611	66604	FL, Poland
66222	DBC, France	66245	DBC, France	66612	66606	FL, Poland
66223	DBC, France	66246	DBC, France	66624	66602	FL, Poland
66225	DBC, France	66247	DBC, France	66625	66601	FL, Poland
66226	DBC, France	66248	DBC, Poland	66954	66019	FL, Poland

Class 86

86213	91 52 00 87703-2	Lancashire Witch	Bulmarket, Bulgaria
86215	91 55 0450 005-8		V-Híd, Hungary
86217	91 55 0450 006-6		V-Híd, Hungary
86218	91 55 0450 004-1		V-Híd, Hungary
86228	91 55 0450 007-4		V-Híd, Hungary
86231	91 52 00 85005-4	Lady of the Lake	Bulmarket, Bulgaria
86232	91 55 0450 003-3		V-Híd, Hungary
86233			Bulmarket, Bulgaria
			(S) Obraztsov Ruse
86234			Bulmarket, Bulgaria
86235	91 52 00 85004-7	Novelty	Bulmarket, Bulgaria
86242	91 55 0450 008-2		V-Híd, Hungary
86248	91 55 0450 001-7		V-Híd, Hungary
86250	91 55 0450 002-5		V-Híd, Hungary
86424	91 55 0450 009-0		V-Híd, Hungary (S) Budapest
86604			Express Service, Obraztsov, Ruse
86605			Express Service, Obraztsov, Ruse
86607			Express Service, Obraztsov, Ruse
86608			Express Service, Obraztsov, Ruse
86609			Express Service, Obraztsov, Ruse
86610			Express Service, Obraztsov, Ruse
86612			Express Service, Obraztsov, Ruse
86613			Express Service, Obraztsov, Ruse
86614			Express Service, Obraztsov, Ruse
86622			Express Service, Obraztsov, Ruse
86627			Express Service, Obraztsov, Ruse
86628			Express Service, Obraztsov, Ruse
86632			Express Service, Obraztsov, Ruse
86637			Express Service, Obraztsov, Ruse

86638			Express Service, Obraztsov, Ruse
86639			Express Service, Obraztsov, Ruse
86701	91 52 00 87701-6	Orion	Bulmarket, Bulgaria
86702	91 52 00 87702-4	Cassiopeia	Bulmarket, Bulgaria

Class 87

87003	91 52 00 87003-7		BZK, Bulgaria
87004	91 52 00 87004-5	Britannia	BZK, Bulgaria
87006	91 52 00 87006-0		BZK, Bulgaria (S) Obraztsov, Ruse
87007	91 52 00 87007-8		BZK, Bulgaria
87008	87008-9		BZK, Bulgaria (S) Obraztsov, Ruse
87009	91 52 00 87009-4		Bulmarket, Bulgaria
87010	91 52 00 87010-2		BZK, Bulgaria (S) Obraztsov, Ruse
87012	91 52 00 87012-8		BZK, Bulgaria
87013	91 52 00 87013-6		BZK, Bulgaria
87014	87014-7		BZK, Bulgaria (S) Obraztsov, Ruse
87017	91 52 00 87017-7	Iron Duke	Bulmarket, Bulgaria
87019	91 52 00 87019-3		BZK, Bulgaria
87020	91 52 00 87020-1		BZK, Bulgaria
87022	91 52 00 87022-7		BZK, Bulgaria
87023	91 52 00 87023-5	Velocity	Bulmarket, Bulgaria
87025	91 52 00 87025-0		Bulmarket, Bulgaria
87026	91 52 00 87026-8		BZK, Bulgaria
87028	91 52 00 87028-4		BZK, Bulgaria
87029	91 52 00 87029-2		BZK, Bulgaria
87033	91 52 00 87033-4		BZK, Bulgaria
87034	91 52 00 87034-2		BZK, Bulgaria

Class 92

92001	91 53 0 472 002-1	Mircea Eliade	DB Cargo, Romania
92002	91 53 0 472 003-9	Lucian Blaga	Transagent Rail, Croatia
92003	91 53 0 472 007-0	Beethoven	DB Cargo, Romania
92005	91 53 0 472-005-4		Transagent Rail, Croatia
92012	91 53 0 472 001-3	Mihai Eminescu	Transagent Rail, Croatia
92022		Charles Dickens	DB Cargo, Bulgaria (S) Aurubis
92024	91 53 0 472 004-7	Marin Preda	Transagent Rail, Croatia
92025	91 52 1 688 025-1	Oscar Wilde	DB Cargo, Bulgaria
92026	91 53 0 472 008-8	Britten	DB Cargo, Romania
92027	91 52 1 688 027-7	George Eliot	DB Cargo, Bulgaria
92030	91 52 1 688 030-1	Ashford	DB Cargo, Bulgaria
92034	91 52 1 688 034-3	Kipling	DB Cargo, Bulgaria
92039	91 53 0 472 006-2	Eugen Ionescu	DB Cargo, Romania

6. CODES

6.1. LIVERY CODES

Livery codes are used to denote the various liveries carried. It is impossible to list every livery variation which currently exists. In particular, items ignored for this publication include minor colour variations, omission of logos and all numbering, lettering and brandings. Descriptions quoted are thus a general guide only. Logos as appropriate for each livery are normally deemed to be carried. The colour of the lower half of the bodyside is stated first.

AB	Arriva Trains Wales/Welsh Government sponsored dark blue.
AG	Arlington Fleet Services (green).
AI	Aggregate Industries (green, light grey & blue).
AL	Advertising/promotional livery (see class heading for details).
AR	Anglia Railways (turquoise blue with a white stripe).
AW	Arriva Trains Wales or Arriva TrainCare dark & light blue.
AZ	Advenza Freight (deep blue with green Advenza brandings).
B	BR blue.
BL	BR Revised blue with yellow cabs, grey roof, large numbers & logo.
BN	Beacon Rail (blue).
CA	Caledonian Sleeper (dark blue).
CD	Cotswold Rail (silver with blue & red logo).
CE	BR Civil Engineers (yellow & grey with black cab doors & window surrounds).
CM	Chiltern Mainline loco-hauled (two-tone grey & silver with blue stripes).
CS	Colas Rail (yellow, orange & black).
CT	Colas Rail HST (orange with broad black & yellow vertical stripes).
CU	Corus (silver with red logos).
DB	DB Cargo (Deutsche Bahn red with grey roof and solebar).
DC	Devon & Cornwall Railways (metallic silver).
DG	BR Departmental (dark grey with black cab doors & window surrounds).
DI	DRS {Class 68 style} (deep blue & aquamarine with compass logo).
DR	Direct Rail Services (dark blue with light blue or dark grey roof).
DS	Revised Direct Rail Services (dark blue, light blue & green. "Compass" logo).
E	English Welsh & Scottish Railway (maroon bodyside & roof with a broad gold bodyside band).
EA	East Midlands Trains revised HST (dark blue, orange & red).
EB	Eurotunnel (two-tone grey with a broad blue stripe).
EC	Euro Cargo Rail (light grey).
EG	"EWS grey" (as **F** but with large yellow & red EWS logo).
EP	European Passenger Services (two-tone grey with dark blue roof).
ER	East Midlands Railway (purple with white or grey lower bodyside lining).
EX	Europhoenix (silver, blue & red).
F	BR Trainload Freight (two-tone grey with black cab doors & window surrounds. Various logos.
FA	Fastline Freight (grey & black with white & orange stripes).
FB	First Group dark blue.
FE	Railfreight Distribution International (two tone-grey with black cab doors & dark blue roof).

FF   Freightliner grey (two-tone grey with black cab doors & window surrounds. Freightliner logo).

FG   New Freightliner; Genesee & Wyoming style (orange with black & yellow lower bodyside stripes).

FH   Revised Freightliner {PowerHaul} (dark green with yellow ends & a grey stripe/buffer beam).

FL   Freightliner (dark green with yellow cabs).

FO   BR Railfreight (grey bodysides, yellow cabs & red lower bodyside stripe, large BR logo).

FR   Fragonset Railways (black with silver roof & a red bodyside band lined out in white).

G   BR Green (plain green, with white stripe on main line locomotives).

GB   GB Railfreight (blue with orange cantrail & solebar stripes, orange cabs).

GC   Grand Central (all over black with an orange stripe).

GG   BR green (two-tone green).

GL   First Great Western locomotives (green with a gold stripe).

GW   Great Western Railway (TOC) dark green.

GY   Eurotunnel (grey & yellow).

HA   Hanson Quarry Products (dark blue/silver with oxide red roof).

HH   Hanson & Hall (dark grey with green branding)..

HN   Harry Needle Railroad Company (orange with a black roof and solebar).

HU   Hunslet Engine Company (dark blue & orange).

IC   BR InterCity (dark grey/white/red/white).

IE   BR InterCity Executive (yellow/light grey/dark grey with a red stripe).

K   Black.

KB   Knorr-Bremse Rail UK (blue, white & light green).

LC   New LNER Class 91+Mark 4 (oxblood, white & light grey with a red stripe).

LH   BR Loadhaul (black with orange cabsides).

LM   London Midland (white/grey & green with broad black stripe around the windows).

LW   LNWR (grey with a red solebar).

M   Maroon.

ML   BR Mainline Freight (aircraft blue with a silver stripe).

MP   Midland Pullman (nanking blue & white).

MT   Maritime (blue with white lettering).

N   BR Network SouthEast (white & blue with red lower bodyside stripe, grey solebar & cab ends).

O   Non-standard (see class heading for details).

PC   Pullman Car Company (umber & cream with gold lettering lined out in gold).

RA   Rail Adventure (dark grey with light grey cabs and green lettering).

RB   Riviera Trains Oxford blue.

RC   Rail Charter Services (green with a broad silver bodyside stripe).

RG   Rail Operations Group dark green.

RL   RMS Locotec (dark blue with light grey or green cabsides).

RO   Rail Operations Group (dark blue).

RR   Regional Railways (dark blue & grey with light blue & white stripes)..

RS   Railway Support Services (grey with a red solebar).

RX   Rail Express Systems (dark grey & red with or without blue markings).

RZ   Royal Train revised (plain claret, no lining).

SL   Silverlink (indigo blue with white stripe, green lower body & yellow doors).

SI	ScotRail InterCity (light grey & dark blue with INTER7CITY branding).
SN	Southern (white & dark green with light green semi-circles at one end of each vehicle. Light grey band at solebar level).
ST	Stagecoach (blue with red cabs).
TB	Transport for Wales all over black with a red logo.
TP	TransPennine Express (silver, grey, blue & purple).
TW	Transport for Wales (white with a red cantrail stripe and grey lower bodyside stripe).
U	Undercoat.
VE	Virgin Trains East Coast (red & white with black window surrounds).
VN	Belmond Northern Belle (crimson lake & cream lined out in gold).
WA	Wabtec Rail (black).
WC	West Coast Railway Company maroon.
XC	CrossCountry (two-tone silver with deep crimson ends and pink doors).
Y	Network Rail yellow.

6.2. OWNER CODES

The following codes are used to define the ownership details of the locomotives or rolling stock listed in this book. Codes shown indicate either the legal owner or "responsible custodian" of each vehicle.

125	125 Group		DT	The Diesel Traction Group
20	Class 20189		E	Eversholt Rail (UK)
37	Scottish Thirty-Seven Group		ED	Ed Murray & Sons
40	Class 40 Preservation Society		EE	English Electric Preservation
47	Stratford 47 Group		EM	East Midlands Railway
50	Class 50 Alliance		EO	ElectroMotive Diesel Services
56	Class 56 Locomotives		EP	Europhoenix
70	7029 Clun Castle		ER	Eastern Rail Services
71	71A Locomotives		ET	Eurotunnel
2L	Class Twenty Locomotives		EU	Eurostar International
A	Angel Trains		EY	European Metal Recycling
AD	AV Dawson		FG	First Group
AF	Arlington Fleet Services		FL	Freightliner
AK	Akiem		GB	GB Railfreight
AM	Alstom UK		GW	Great Western Railway
AV	Arriva UK Trains		HH	Hanson & Hall Rail Services
BD	Bardon Aggregates		HN	Harry Needle Railroad Company
BN	Beacon Rail		HX	Halifax Bank of Scotland
CD	Crewe Diesel Preservation Group		LF	Lombard Finance
			LL	Llanelli & Mynydd Mawr Railway
CS	Colas Rail		LN	London Overground
D0	D05 Preservation Group		LO	LORAM (UK)
DA	Data Acquisition & Testing Services		LS	Locomotive Services
			ME	Meteor Power
DB	DB Cargo (UK)		MR	Mendip Rail
DC	DC Rail		NB	Boden Rail Engineering
DE	Diesel and Electric Preservation Group		NM	National Museum of Science & Industry
DP	Deltic Preservation Society		NR	Network Rail
DR	Direct Rail Services		NS	Nemesis Rail

NY	North Yorkshire Moors Railway Enterprises	RU	Russell Logistics
P	Porterbrook Leasing Company	SB	Steve Beniston
PG	Progress Rail UK Leasing	SP	The Scottish Railway Preservation Society
PO	Other private owner	ST	Shaun Wright
PP	Peter Pan Locomotive Company	SU	SembCorp Utilities UK
RA	Rail Adventure	TW	Transport for Wales
RL	Rail Management Services (trading as RMS Locotec)	UR	UK Rail Leasing
		VG	Victoria Group
RO	Rail Operations Group	VT	Vintage Trains
RS	Railway Support Services	WC	West Coast Railway Company
RV	Riviera Trains	WM	West Midlands Trains

6.3. LOCOMOTIVE POOL CODES

Locomotives are split into operational groups ("pools") for diagramming and maintenance purposes. The codes used to denote these pools are shown in this publication.

AWCA	West Coast Railway Company operational locomotives.
AWCX	West Coast Railway Company stored locomotives.
CFOL	Class 50 Operations locomotives.
CFSL	Class 40 Preservation Society Locomotives.
COFS	Colas Rail Classes 37 & 56.
COLO	Colas Rail Classes 66 & 70.
COLS	Colas Rail stored locomotives.
COTS	Colas Rail Classes 37 & 43.
DCRO	DC Rail operational locomotives.
DCRS	DC Rail stored locomotives.
DFGI	Freightliner Class 70.
DFHG	Freightliner Class 59.
DFHH	Freightliner Class 66/6.
DFIM	Freightliner Class 66/5.
DFIN	Freightliner low emission Class 66.
DFLC	Freightliner Class 90.
DFLH	Freightliner Class 47.
DHLT	Freightliner locomotives awaiting maintenance/repair/disposal.
EFOO	Great Western Railway Class 57.
EFPC	Great Western Railway Class 43.
EHPC	CrossCountry Class 43.
EPEX	Europhoenix UK stored locomotives.
EPUK	Europhoenix UK locomotives.
ERSL	Eastern Rail Services locomotives.
GBBS	GB Railfreight Class 57.
GBBT	GB Railfreight Class 66. Large fuel tanks.
GBCS	GB Railfreight Class 73/9. Caledonian Sleeper.
GBCT	GB Railfreight Class 92. Channel Tunnel traffic.
GBDF	GB Railfreight Class 47.
GBEB	GB Railfreight Class 66. Ex-European, large fuel tanks.
GBED	GB Railfreight Class 73.
GBEL	GB Railfreight Class 66. New build, small fuel tanks.

GBFM	GB Railfreight Class 66. RETB fitted.
GBGD	GB Railfreight Class 56. Operational locomotives.
GBHH	GB Railfreight Class 66. Regeared locomotives.
GBKP	GB Railfreight Class 67.
GBLT	GB Railfreight Class 66. Small fuel tanks.
GBNB	GB Railfreight Class 66. New build.
GBNR	GB Railfreight Class 73/9. Network Rail contracts.
GBOB	GB Railfreight Class 66. Former DB Cargo locomotives; large fuel tanks and buckeye couplers.
GBRG	GB Railfreight Class 69.
GBSD	GB Railfreight. Stored locomotives.
GBSL	GB Railfreight Class 92. Caledonian Sleeper.
GBST	GB Railfreight Class 92. Caledonian Sleeper & Channel Tunnel.
GBTG	GB Railfreight Class 60.
GBYH	GB Railfreight Class 59.
GBZZ	GB Railfreight locomotives for disposal.
GROG	Rail Operations Group diesel locomotives.
HAPC	ScotRail Class 43.
HHPC	Rail Adventure Class 43.
HNRL	Harry Needle Railroad Company hire locomotives.
HNRS	Harry Needle Railroad Company stored locomotives.
HTLX	Hanson & Hall Rail Services locomotives.
HVAC	Hanson & Hall Rail Services Class 50.
HYWD	South Western Railway Class 73.
ICHP	125 Group Class 43.
IECA	London North Eastern Railway Class 91.
IECP	London North Eastern Railway Class 43 (stored).
LRLO	LORAM locomotives.
LSLO	Locomotive Services operational locomotives.
LSLS	Locomotive Services stored locomotives.
MBDL	Non TOC-owned diesel locomotives.
MBED	Non TOC-owned electro-diesel locomotives.
MBEL	Non TOC-owned electric locomotives.
MOLO	Class 20189 Ltd Class 20.
NRLO	Nemesis Rail locomotives.
QADD	Network Rail locomotives.
QCAR	Network Rail New Measurement Train Class 43.
QETS	Network Rail Class 37.
RAJV	Scottish Railway Preservation Society Class 37.
SAXL	Eversholt Rail off-lease locomotives.
SBXL	Porterbrook Leasing Company stored locomotives.
SCEL	Angel Trains stored locomotives.
SROG	Rail Operations Group stored locomotives
TPEX	TransPennine Express Class 68 locomotives.
UKRL	UK Rail Leasing. Operational locomotives.
UKRM	UK Rail Leasing. Locomotives for overhaul.
UKRS	UK Rail Leasing. Stored locomotives.
WAAC	DB Cargo Class 67.
WAEC	DB Cargo Class 67. Fitted with ETCS.
WAWC	DB Cargo Class 67 for hire to Transport for Wales.
WBAE	DB Cargo Class 66. Locomotives fitted with "stop-start" technology.

WBAI	DB Cargo Class 66. Locomotives returned from DB Cargo Rail France.
WBAK	DB Cargo Class 66. ETCS fitted.
WBAR	DB Cargo Class 66. Fitted with remote monitoring equipment.
WBAT	DB Cargo Class 66.
WBBE	DB Cargo Class 66. RETB fitted and fitted with "stop-start" technology.
WBBT	DB Cargo Class 66. RETB fitted.
WBET	DB Cargo Class 66. Fitted with ETCS.
WBLE	DB Cargo Class 66. Dedicated locomotives for Lickey Incline banking duties. Fitted with "stop-start" technology.
WBRT	DB Cargo Class 66. Locomotives dedicated to autumn RHTT trains.
WCAT	DB Cargo Class 60.
WCBT	DB Cargo Class 60. Extended-range fuel tanks.
WEAC	DB Cargo Class 90.
WEDC	DB Cargo Class 90. Modified for operation with Mark 4s.
WFAC	DB Cargo Class 92.
WFBC	DB Cargo Class 92 with TVM430 cab signalling equipment for use on High Speed 1.
WQAA	DB Cargo stored locomotives Group 1A (short-term maintenance).
WQAB	DB Cargo stored locomotives Group 1B.
WQBA	DB Cargo stored locomotives Group 2 (unserviceable).
WQCA	DB Cargo stored locomotives Group 3 (unserviceable).
WQDA	DB Cargo stored locomotives Group 4 (awaiting disposal or for sale).
XHAC	Direct Rail Services Class 57/3.
XHCE	Direct Rail Services Class 68 for hire to Chiltern Railways.
XHCS	Direct Rail Services Class 68 for hire to Chiltern Railways (spare locomotives).
XHIM	Direct Rail Services locomotives – Intermodal traffic.
XHSO	Direct Rail Services Supply Chain Operations locomotives.
XHTP	Direct Rail Services Class 68 for hire to TransPennine Express (spare locomotives).
XHVE	Direct Rail Services Classes 68 & 88.
XHVT	Direct Rail Services Class 57/3 for hire to Avanti West Coast.
XSDP	Direct Rail Services locomotives for disposal.
XWSS	Direct Rail Services stored locomotives.

6.4. ALLOCATION & LOCATION CODES

Allocation codes are used in this publication to denote the normal maintenance base ("depots") of each operational locomotive. However, maintenance may be carried out at other locations and also by mobile teams. The designation (S) denotes stored.

Code	Location	Depot Operator
BH	Barrow Hill (Chesterfield)	Barrow Hill Engine Shed Society
BL	Shackerstone, Battlefield Line	*Storage location only*
BM	Bournemouth	South Western Railway
BO	Bo'ness (West Lothian)	The Bo'ness & Kinneil Railway
BQ	Bury (Greater Manchester)	East Lancashire Railway Trust
BU	Burton-on-Trent	Nemesis Rail
CB	Crewe Basford Hall	Freightliner Engineering
CE	Crewe International	DB Cargo (UK)

CF	Cardiff Canton	Transport for Wales
CL	Crewe LNWR Heritage	LNWR Heritage Company
CO	Coquelles (France)	Eurotunnel
CQ	Crewe Heritage Centre	Crewe Heritage Trust
CR	Crewe Gresty Bridge	Direct Rail Services
CS	Carnforth	West Coast Railway Company
CT	Cheriton (Folkestone)	Eurotunnel
EC	Edinburgh Craigentinny	Hitachi
EP	Ely Papworth Sidings	*Storage location only*
HA	Haymarket (Edinburgh)	ScotRail
HO	Hope Cement Works	Breedon Hope Cement
HJ	Hoo Junction (Kent)	Colas Rail
KI	King's Norton (Birmingham)	SLC Operations
KM	Carlisle Kingmoor	Direct Rail Services
KR	Kidderminster	Severn Valley Railway
LA	Laira (Plymouth)	Great Western Railway
LB	Loughborough Works	UK Rail Leasing
LD	Leeds Midland Road	Freightliner Engineering
LR	Leicester	UK Rail Leasing
LT	Longport (Stoke-on-Trent)	ElectroMotive Diesel Services
MD	Merehead	Mendip Rail
MG	Margate One:One Collection	Locomotive Services
NL	Neville Hill (Leeds)	Northern
NM	Nottingham Eastcroft	East Midlands Railway/Boden Rail
NY	Grosmont (North Yorkshire)	North Yorkshire Moors Railway Enterprises
OD	RIDC Melton (Old Dalby)	Network Rail
PG	Peterborough	GB Railfreight
PZ	Penzance Long Rock	Great Western Railway
RD	Ruddington (Nottingham Heritage Rly)	125 Group
RO	Rowsley (Derbyshire)	Park Rail
RR	Doncaster Robert's Road	ElectroMotive Diesel Services
RU	Rugby	Colas Rail
SC	Scunthorpe Steelworks	British Steel
SE	St Leonards (Hastings)	St Leonards Railway Engineering
SK	Swanwick West (Derbyshire)	The Princess Royal Locomotive Trust
SW	Swanage	Swanage Railway
TM	Tyseley Locomotive Works	Vintage Trains
TN	Tonbridge	GB Railfreight
TO	Toton (Nottinghamshire)	DB Cargo (UK)
WB	Wembley (London)	Alstom UK
WS	Worksop (Nottinghamshire)	Harry Needle Railroad Company
YA	Great Yarmouth	Eastern Rail Services
YK	National Railway Museum (York)	National Museum of Science & Industry
ZA	RTC Business Park (Derby)	LORAM (UK)
ZB	Doncaster Works	Wabtec Rail
ZD	Derby Works	Alstom UK
ZG	Eastleigh Works	Arlington Fleet Services
ZI	Ilford Works	Alstom UK
ZJ	Stoke-on-Trent Works	Axiom Rail (Stoke)
ZK	Kilmarnock Works	Brodie Engineering
ZN	Wolverton Works	Gemini Rail Group
ZR	Holgate Works (York)	Network Rail